THE CAREER OF ROBERT NEWELL

OREGON PIONEER

By

GEORGE GUY DELAMARTER

A THESIS*

Presented to the Department of History
and the Graduate School of the University of Oregon
in partial fulfillment of the requirements for the degree of
Master of Science

June 1951

*Original format kept intact and not edited to contemporary standards of scholarship.

The Career of Robert Newell Oregon Pioneer
© 2005 Newell House Museum

Published by the Newell House Museum
under the auspices of the Champoeg Buildings and Grounds Committee
Oregon State Society, National Society Daughters of the American Revolution

Manufactured in the United States by Newport LazerQuick
in conjunction with Dancing Moon Press, Newport, Oregon
through generous donations made by
the author, George Guy Delamarter and West Coast Bank.

Book Design by Judy A. Van Atta
Cover photo and layout by Andrew E. Cier
Cover photo of Robert Newell courtesy of Champoeg State Heritage Area, Champoeg, Oregon

ISBN: 978-1-892076-18-2
Library of Congress Control Number: 2005932341
Delamarter, George Guy
"The Career of Robert Newell Oregon Pioneer"
 1.   Title; 2. Oregon History; 3. Biography

To order additional copies write:
Newell House Museum
8089 Champoeg Rd. NE
Saint Paul, Oregon 97137

First Edition
2005

FOREWORD

Students of Oregon's early history will find surprisingly few references to Robert "Doc" Newell, considering the size of the role that he actually played. Some of those references use the word "remarkable" in their brief descriptions. Newell's life was indeed remarkable, and a book chronicling his life is long overdue.

George Guy Delamarter has done an outstanding job meticulously combing through the journals, letters, diaries, newspapers and public records to piece together the story of a man fellow pioneers described as brave, honest and kindhearted, an "unquestioned leader" who exerted great influence on the development of the Pacific Northwest. Delamarter follows Newell's career, beginning with the hazardous life of a fur trapper, his early attempts at farming, and his numerous entrepreneurial adventures. He then takes the reader on a journey through the inner workings of the evolution of Oregon's political system, providing insights on the issues of the day, back-slapping and back-stabbing alliances, and why Robert Newell was all but written out of the early books on Oregon history.

In his final years, Newell returned to Idaho—scene of his fur-trapping days—and attempted to aid the Nez Perce Indians in negotiating a reasonable treaty. Delamarter chronicles the issues faced by settlers and Indians when trying to live with each other, as well as Newell's unique perspective and understanding of the Indians' viewpoints. The reader will see that if the government had paid more attention to the advice of Robert Newell, much bloodshed may have been avoided.

"The Career of Robert Newell—Oregon Pioneer" is recommended reading for students of Oregon history wanting an in-depth look at the life and times of a pioneer who played a part in so many aspects of the settlement of the Oregon Country.

Dennis Wiley, Manager
Champoeg State Heritage Area

ACKNOWLEDGMENTS

Giving birth to a book—from idea to final copy—is quite a process, and many people helped along the way. This process could not have been completed without the assistance of the following:

Al LePage, Living History Interpreter portraying Robert Newell, who investigated and promoted the possibilities of publishing the book.

Judy A. Van Atta, Caretaker, Robert Newell House Museum, who undertook the daunting task of typing the entire original master's thesis on the computer, and also collected and chose the images and photographs for the book. Additionally she worked with Joan A. Hunter, State Regent, Oregon State Society, NSDAR, and Rose R. Reed of Newport LazerQuick to organize and craft the final copy.

Andrew E. Cier, who designed the cover layout using his own photography along with the existing portrait of Robert Newell.

Bill Buckingham, Caretaker, Pioneer Mother's Memorial Cabin, who proofed the final text.

Dennis Wiley, Oregon Parks and Recreations Department Manager, Champoeg State Heritage Area, who provided encouragement, advice, photographs, and wrote the Foreword.

West Coast Bank and David Hansen, Vice President, Portland/Vancouver area, whose generous donation funded the illustrations, representing both their continued commitment to the museum and investment in the local community.

To the staff of the Salem Public Library, the Oregon Historical Society's research library and the Statesman Journal for assisting in the research and providing the images and photographs included in the book.

We are indebted to Guy Delamarter, who researched and wrote the master's thesis as a University of Oregon student under the tutelage of professor Dr. Dan Clark, and for his willingness to agree to its publication, as well as donating the rights of his manuscript to the museum. Through their generous donation, Guy and his wife Dorthy, have made possible the first printing. The monies generated from the sale of this book will be used for future printings, as needed, and specifically to fund in perpetuity the interpretation of Robert Newell through the museum for present and future generations.

TABLE OF CONTENTS

TABLE OF ILLUSTRATIONS

PREFACE

The life of Robert Newell was chosen for study because of the prominent part he played in the early history of Oregon, and because his importance has generally been overlooked. Secondary authors, if they mention him at all, usually pass over his life by noting that he was an early Oregon settler and a friend of Joe Meek. The attention which has been focused on Joe Meek has robbed some of his contemporaries of due consideration. It is the author's firm conviction that Robert Newell was Meek's superior in character and in the influence he exerted upon the formation and early years of Oregon government. The newspapers of the time indicate that Newell held a commanding position in the community which Meek never approached. W. J. Ghent, in his article on Newell in the Dictionary of American Biography, states that with the death of Ewing Young, Newell assumed leadership in the affairs of the Oregon country which he maintained for several years. In his private financial affairs Newell was comparatively well-to-do (certainly a contrast to Meek), until the flood of the Willamette River in 1861-62 claimed many of his assets.

Doubtless the paucity of references to Newell in secondary works compared to the attention Meek has received arises from the popularization of the latter as a result of Mrs. Victor's River of the West in which Joe Meek is the hero. Meek has become the epitome of all the characteristics which we attribute to the Oregon Pioneers. Many things have been attributed to Meek which could just as surely have been ascribed to Newell or others of the pioneers.

Because the secondary writers have written so little about Newell the writer has obtained the material pertinent to Newell's life from the journals, ledgers, diaries and letters of those who knew him, and from the contemporary newspapers and records which mention his name.

To obtain this material the writer with the assistance of Mr. Schmidt, Curator of the Oregon Collection, has contacted the following libraries and collections: Bancroft collection, Huntington library, University of Indiana library, Library of Congress, the State library at Salem, the library at Lewiston College, Lewiston, Idaho, where Newell spent the last years of his life, and the library of Yale University.

The University of Oregon library has in its Oregon collection a microfilm copy of the original diary which Newell kept while hunting and trapping in the mountains. This diary covers the years 1829 through 1842.

The Oregon Historical Society at Portland has a great deal of material essential to this study. The provisional and territorial papers of Oregon contain many references to Newell and valuable information regarding his part in the formation of the government. Also a great many diaries, letters and manuscripts without which a thorough understanding of Newell would have been impossible.

Newell left two diaries besides the one mentioned. One written in 1848 while he was a peace commissioner to the Indians east of the Cascades, and the other a record of his trip to Washington, D. C., in which he accompanied four Nez Perce Indian Chiefs with Mr. James O'Neil (Indian Agent of the Idaho Territory) to the nation's capital to aid in securing amendments to an Indian treaty of 1863. The Diary of 1848 has not been available. The Bancroft library was unable to locate it and the one owned by the state of Oregon was burned in the capitol fire. A copy of the diary of 1868 is on file at the Oregon Historical Society in Portland.

Perhaps the most fruitful source of information regarding controversial issues is the correspondence of the Herald, a newspaper printed in Portland in the 1860's. The Historical Society at Portland possesses the original correspondence which is apparently in the handwriting of Newell and written to answer the articles written by W. H. Gray published in the Astoria Marine Gazette. Much of the argument between the two is personalized and of little value historically, but parts are valuable source material in which many early incidents are discussed.

Most Oregonians are familiar with the historical marker at Champoeg on which are the names of those who voted to organize a provisional government in 1843. The name of Robert Newell is of course inscribed on the marker. Outside of this one inscription the author was unable to find any reference to Newell in the park whose memorial building is lined with pictures and remembrances of other pioneers, yet Newell was almost the reason for the existence of Champoeg. He caused the town to be plotted and he placed the first keel-boats in the Willamette above Oregon City to transport wheat from Champoeg to the falls at Oregon City. He also owned a store and flour mill in Champoeg. He owned the ground on which the memorial park is now situated for many years. If through this humble effort those interested in early Oregon history will come to appreciate Robert Newell for what he was the writer will feel his work has not been in vain.

Newell was not a great leader in the same sense as some of our national leaders or even our more important state leaders of later years such as J. W. Nesmith, Joseph Lane or Asahel Bush. He was poorly educated and as more people came to Oregon he was not able to influence the electorate by the dictatorial methods which Bush used so successfully, nor was he as universally popular as Lane and Nesmith. But considering his background which seemed to fit him for little more than fighting Indians, his career is a fine tribute to his ability to adapt himself to the needs of the time.

It has been the writer's purpose to present the facts as accurately as possible after examining the original documents.

The author would like to express thanks to Dr. Dan Clark, head of the history department of the University of Oregon, for his kind suggestions and unerring advice; Inez Haskel and Priscilla Knuth, of the staff of the Oregon Historical Society, for their untiring aid in finding the needed material; Mr. Schmidt for his able assistance in corresponding with other libraries, and my wife for her assistance in orthography and correcting syntax.

CHAPTER I

EARLY LIFE: TRAPPER AND HUNTER

Robert Newell was born into the era of "manifest destiny" near Zanesville, Ohio, on March 30, 1807. Information about his early life or parentage, like that on many another "mountain man," seems to have been obscured or forgotten. Newell himself, though in later life he wrote a great deal of material which is valuable historically, evaded personal references to a large extent. The circumstances surrounding his early life which can be found in his own writing are quite insignificant. One historian says that Newell left Ohio for St. Louis where he became an apprentice in a saddle shop. His father died when the boy was eighteen, [1] leaving him to make his way as he could.

Newell's formal education was not extensive, to judge by the many grammatical errors and misspelled words in his writings. But he must have been blessed with good home training, "...else we cannot account for the qualities of restraint and control and the natural leadership which made him so useful..."[2]

Four years after the death of his father, possibly because of a love of adventure, Newell joined a trapping and trading expedition bound for the upper waters of Green River. While on this expedition he kept a diary recording his whereabouts during the ten years he spent in trapping and trading.

> March 9, 1829, I left St. Louis with Mr. William Sublette, who was the proprietor of our camp, on a hunting expedition for beever. Fifty four men in all, arrived at the foot of the mountains on Sweetwater the 17th of July, where we met his hunters or a part, and crossed the mountains from the waters of the Missouri

---

[1] Hulbert Howe Bancroft, History of Oregon, 2 vols. (San Francisco: 1888), I:244.

[2] T. C. Elliott, "Doctor Robert Newell: Pioneer," Oregon Historical Quarterly, IX (March 1908), 104.

to the Columbia, and Prier's Fork we fell in with M. Smith and Jackson partners of Wm. Sublette. On August 20th held randervois and separated for beever hunting when all together about 175 men.[3]

If Newell joined the party in search of adventure, he was not disappointed. For the next ten years he traveled back and forth across the mountains and plains and was constantly in danger of being attacked by Indians or wild animals. The scrimmages of the trappers and pioneers with the hostile Indians of the plains and Rocky Mountain areas form an exciting chapter in the history of the West.

Newell was twenty-two when he joined the expedition, and with Joe Meek, a member at the tender age of eighteen, was evidently conspicuous for his youth. One morning while the company was camped in central Missouri, Newell and Meek were out rounding up the mules. Newell made some cursory remarks about an old lady who was returning from the milking yard. He spoke so loudly that the old lady overheard him, and she snapped back with: "Young chap I'll bet you run off from your mother! Who'll mend them holes in the elbo of your coat? Your a pretty looking chap to go to the mountains among them Injuns! They'll kill you. You better go back home."[4]

Undaunted by the advice of the frontier woman, who no doubt felt sorry for the young fellows, Joe Meek and Robert Newell not only continued on with the expedition, they spent ten years as trappers, much of the time as companions in the wilderness.

The life of a fur trapper was a hazardous one. Outnumbered by hostile Indians, subject to extreme weather conditions, and frequently without food supplies except game, it took a combination of persuasiveness and strong physical talents to be one of the surviving "fittest." The most daring exploits were necessary to keep the supplies and horses out of Indian hands. In 1831 a party of Crow Indians succeeded in driving off three hundred head of horses

---

[3] Newell Diary, 1829. The University of Oregon Library has a photo static copy of the original diary. For a biographical sketch of William Sublette and his fur interests see Hiram M. Chittenden, The American Fur Trade of the Far West, 2 vols. (New York: Francis P. Harper, 1902), I: 252.
[4] Frances Fuller Victor, River of the West (Hartford, Conn.: Columbia Book Co., 1870), p. 44.

which were necessary for the success of the expedition. In that particular party were two hundred men.[5] It was decided to send one hundred trappers on foot to catch the thieves and retake the horses. Among those chosen for this risky expedition were Joe Meek and Robert Newell. After 200 miles of night and day tracking, the trappers located both horses and horse thieves near a branch of the Big Horn River. They took their position on a bluff opposite the Indian camp, and while the Indians were "wrapped in a satisfied slumber, Robert Newell and Antoine Godin crept into the Indian hideout and drove off the horses. The Indians were aroused by the running horses but when they arose to stop the trampling steeds, a volley of shots by the trappers on the bluff so confused them that the whites made good the recovery of their animals."[6]

Often the fur companies sent a man to the Indians to make peace. Newell at various times was delegated to approach these unfriendly Indians and secure their good will, a large item in the trapper's chance of success. It was impossible to predict just what kind of a reception the peace delegate would receive, for the Indians were savage and treacherous. Newell's diary indicates that some of those sent out to bargain did not return alive: "Mr. Tullock sent a man on express to the Crows, as he has stayed 20 days over his time we think he is killed."[7]

Newell very nearly lost his life on one such expedition. "As the Crows had committed so many depredations on the whites heretofore by killing and robbing it was their intention to send me with a small supply of goods to induce them to let the whites pass in peace."[8] The diary does not record the exciting events of this mission, but Newell told his experience to Peter H. Burnett, who

---

[5] Newell's Diary has the following short note indicating a change of employers: "This Summer 1830 Mr. Smith, Jackson and Sublette sold out and left the country. Their successors were Mr. Fitzpatrick, M. Sublette, Freab, Garvis and J. Bridger. Our squad now consists of about 200 men."

[6] Victor, River of the West, p. 98.
[7] Newell Diary, 1829.
[8] Ibid.
[9] Osborne Russell, Journal of a Trapper (Boise, Idaho: Syms-York Company, 1921), p. 146.

preserved the story in this <u>Recollections And Opinions of An Old Pioneer.</u> In his "slow hesitating way" Newell told the following story of his mission to the Crow Indians.

Newell had asked the Missouri Fur Company, his employer, to supply him with an interpreter and a cook. With these two men Newell made his way to the Crow Camp. The Crow Indians "are proud, treacherous, thievish, insolent and brave when they are possessed with a superior advantage, but when placed in the opposite situation they are equally humble, submissive and cowardly."[9] The Indian chief called a council of all the chiefs to meet Newell and the interpreter. The spokesman for the Crows entered the council with a large bundle of sticks. When all was quiet the Indian orator began by recounting the evil deeds, which the whites had committed against the Indians. For each wrong mentioned the Indian would lay aside one of the sticks until he had exhausted the bundle. For each of the complaints the Indian demanded a certain amount of merchandise as reparation.

During this impressive speech Newell was quite overwhelmed. He was not prepared to balance this long list of depredations by similar charges against the Indians. He knew that the amount of merchandize demanded was beyond the ability of the company to pay. He determined to change the line of thought upon which the council had been proceeding. Newell told the council that he was only the agent of the company and was not authorized to make any stipulation for payment to either party; that both parties were guilty of wrong deeds and no one could be sure which party had done the most or was the most to blame and that he had come to bury the past to bring peace in the future. The chiefs were impressed by this bold frankness and agreed to a treaty.

Newell might well have congratulated himself on his success, but an incident occurred shortly after this council, which not only endangered the peace agreement but very nearly, cost him his life. In the evening the cook hung a small kettle above the fire and filled it with fat buffalo meat. While the cook was gone the kettle boiled over and Newell, who was visiting a short distance away in one of the lodges of a chief, saw the fat meat burst into

---

[9] Osborne Russell, <u>Journal of a Trapper</u> (Boise, Idaho: Syms-York Company, 1921), p. 146.

flames. His first concern was to prevent the lodge and possibly the entire encampment from burning. He ran to his lodge, seized the kettle and threw it away from the lodge. The contents struck an Indian in the face and burned him severely. The poor savage gave a loud scream, which instantly aroused the entire camp. It appeared that the Indian's eyes had been burned so that he could not see. As the Indians apprehended the cause of the accident, they began a vehement demand for punishment. The head chief summoned a council to decide what should be done. The chiefs took their places in the council-lodge, while the rest of the tribe, men, women and children, grouped themselves around the door of the lodge. As Newell and his interpreter made their way through the narrow passage left for them to enter they were greeted with signs of utmost hatred, especially by the women, who would lean away and shrink from Newell as if his touch would contaminate them. As he entered the council-lodge, lighted only by a small fire, all was complete silence. No one moved or spoke for some time. Suddenly the death-like silence was broken by one of the old chiefs who howled like a great wolf, the imitation being almost perfect. More silence followed, then the piercing blood-chilling cry of the panther came from a second chief. Another period of silence and a third chief imitated an enraged grizzly bear. The effect of the procedure was terrifying to say the least. Newell felt that his chances of living to a ripe old age were indeed small.

As Newell watched the chiefs who were to decide his fate, he concluded that all were his enemies but the old man who was the head chief of the tribe. The latter had remained calm throughout the council and apparently understood the situation. He asked Newell to relate the facts to the council truly; under such conditions he thought there might be a chance for him. Newell stated the facts as they had occurred, and his frank manner had a favorable effect. After deliberating most of the night, the council agreed to postpone the case until the extent of the injury could be determined. While the Indian was recuperating, Newell and his companions were not allowed to leave the camp. The Indian improved rapidly and was not as seriously hurt as had been thought.

Newell was anticipating his release from the Crows when one day an Indian horseman was seen signaling to the camp some one hundred yards distant. When he had attracted the attention of the camp, "he dismounted, rolled up his buffalo-robe, took hold of one end of the roll, and slowly and solemnly swung it around his head several times, then he folded it up, and sat upon it, and brought both his open hands slowly down his face several times in succession, the signs were unmistakable. The messenger was sent by another camp of their tribe to inform them that the dreaded disease of smallpox had broken out among them." Newell said the scene which followed depicted sorrow such as he had never before witnessed. The women and children ran through the camp crying and wailing.

Newell had finally regained the confidence of his captors after burning the old Indian, but now they treated him more fiercely then ever because they attributed the outbreak of smallpox to the trappers. Smallpox was feared much more than war and the Indians anticipated the horrible results of the scourge. Since the disease was unknown until the white man came, they naturally blamed him for its presence. They thronged around Newell and his companions and probably would have killed them on the spot, but again the old chief intervened. Saying that it was useless to weep and lament, he mounted his horse and ordered the camp to be moved to the Wind River Mountains. In less than an hour the Indians were moving toward their new camp. Newell says: "The fear of that complaint (smallpox) set them running from it so very hard it wore out several hundred horses before we stopped the retreat."[10] Game and good weather were abundant in their new location and the excitement and alarm soon were forgotten. With vigilance relaxed, Newell was at last allowed to depart. Not one case of smallpox developed, or his life might not have been spared.[11]

The winter of 1832 was spent with the Nez Perce and Flathead Indians,[12] and it is probable that he met his future wife in this year. He was married to the daughter of a Nez Perce sub-chief, probably in 1833. He does not mention the event in his diary, though there is recorded the birth of his first child, Francis Newell,

---

[10] Newell Diary, 1829.

[11] I have followed the account of Peter H. Burnett, Recollections and Opinions of an Old Pioneer (New York: D. Appleton and Co., 1880), pp. 163-168.

[12] Newell Diary, 1829. For a history of the Nez Perce see Kate C. McBeth, The Nez Perces Since Lewis and Clark (New York: Fleming H. Revell Company, 1908). This book deals largely with the missionary activity among the Indians but it also contains much reliable material pertaining to their culture.

on the 14th of June, 1835.[13]   His Indian wife was a faithful companion throughout the remainder of Newell's adventures in the mountains, and accompanied him to the Willamette Valley when Newell settled down as a farmer. Newell refers to her in his diary as "My woman," never mentioning her as his wife.

The friendship begun in 1832 between Newell and the Nez Perce Indians resulted in important consequences. He was always fair and honest in his association with the Indians, a policy which paid him dividends in his latter years when he needed their help. The goodwill planted in this year lasted until Newell's death in 1869.

All the Indians were not as friendly as the Nez Perce. The Blackfeet especially were hostile and are mentioned in Newell's diary many times as causing trouble because of their fierce, nefarious nature.[14]   In a skirmish with them in 1836, Newell dismounted to scalp an Indian who had been shot and was supposedly dead. He had seized the long black hair of the savage with one hand and with his knife in the other made a pass at the Indian, when the latter suddenly came to his senses and gave battle. For a time it seemed that Newell would lose his own scalp, but he finally managed to free himself and mounted his horse—minus the Indian scalp, but happy to be in possession of his own.

In spite of the danger involved these trappers seemed to enjoy their fights with the Indians. In 1837 Newell arrived at a camp where the whites were in battle with the Bannock Indians. He mentions the incident as follows: "…we found the Whites engaged with the Banock Indians fighting. We joined the sport…"[15]

---

[13] Newell Diary, 1829. Mrs. Victor in <u>River of the West</u>, p. 253, says that Meek married one of the Nez Perce women in 1838, but had trouble getting the chief's consent. T. C. Elliott, <u>op. cit.</u>, p. 106, states that the two girls, Meek's wife and Newell's wife, were of the same family. Harvey E. Tobie, the latest biographer of Meek, agrees. <u>No Man Like Joe</u> (Portland, Oregon: Binford and Mort, 1949), p. 76.

[14] For a description of the Blackfeet Indians see George Catlin, <u>The Manners Customs and Condition of the North American Indians.</u> 2 Vols. (Picadilly London: published by the Author at the Egyptian Hall, 1841), I:29-54. Also <u>The Life Letters and Travels of Father Pierre-Jean De Smet.</u> 4 Vols. Ed. by H. M. Chittenden and A. T. Richardson (New York: Francis P. Harper, 1905), III: 946-936.

[15] Newell Diary, 1829.

Fighting Indians and trapping beaver were the most important duties of these mountain men. More in the nature of amusement was the "rendezvous," a designated meeting-place at which the trappers assembled at least once a year. "Each summer usually at some meadow in the vicinity of Green River two weeks or more were spent in conference balancing of accounts and trading by the proprietors and in sports and dissipation by the large majority of reckless trappers and servants, American, British and friendly Indians…"[16] If not a wholesome experience, the wild celebration which occurred was at least a diversion from the routine rigors of the life.

Differing from the British custom, the American fur companies seldom established posts beyond the mountains. Their business transactions usually were regulated by partners who often traveled extensively in the area from which the furs were taken. These partners moved about from place to place, endeavoring to monopolize the fur trade with the Indians. Various groups of trappers were sent into specially assigned areas to hunt and trap for the company. Sometime during the summer, when the furs were not at their best and there was an interval between the hunting seasons, the various groups of trappers, the partners of the fur companies, and a miscellaneous body of free trappers and friendly Indians gathered with the products of the year's campaign. To this rendezvous the company sent supplies to outfit the trappers for the next season.

Captain Bonneville's account of the rendezvous gives us an interesting insight into the festivities of one such occasion. There were "contests of skill at running, jumping, wrestling, shooting with the rifle and running horses….They drank together, they sang, they laughed, they whooped, they tried to outbrag and outlie each other in stories of their adventures and achievements."[17]

The arrival of the supplies gave the regular finish to
the annual revel. A grand outbreak of wild debauch

---

[16] T. C. Elliott, "Doctor Robert Newell, Mountain Man," in Oregon Voter, a magazine printed weekly in Portland, Oregon, F. H. Young and C. C. Chapman, editors, August 20, 1927, pp. 14-15.
[17] Washington Irving, The Rocky Mountains: Digested from the Journal of Captain B. L. E. Bonneville, 2 Vols. (Philadelphia: Carey, Lea and Blanchard, 1837), I:202.

ensued among the mountaineers; drinking, dancing, swaggering, gambling, quarrelling and fighting . . . alchohol is dealt out to the trappers at four dollars a pint. When inflamed by this fiery beverage they cut all kinds of mad pranks and gambals and sometimes burn all their clothes in their drunken bravadoes. A camp recovering from one of these riotous revels presents a serio-comic spectacle;   black eyes, broken heads, lackluster visages. Many trappers have squandered in one drunken frolic the hard-earned wages of a year . . . .[18]

In such a reckless atmosphere the trappers forgot—if they ever knew—the restraints of organized society. Four trappers playing cards on the dead body of a comrade exemplifies the lack of propriety exhibited.[19]

Following the festivities of the rendezvous the parties separated to work again their respective trapping areas. Each group endeavored to provide themselves with enough provisions for the winter, but bad weather, Indian thievery, and scarcity of game at times placed the men in difficult straits. Newell related one such incident in 1861, several years after he had given up the life of a trapper.

Newell was one of a party of hunters numbering between sixty and ninety men. After hunting parts of the Snake, Flathead, Nez Perce and Blackfeet areas, the party noticed that game was unusually scarce. Consequently they determined to cross the mountains in search of buffalo and to erect quarters for the winter there. Since provisions were low before they started across the mountains, they were starving within a short time. To make matters worse, heavy snow covered what little grass there was for the horses. With even the best hunters unsuccessful, "the men began to talk of younger days—of the old stump at the end of the lane near the school-house—the chicken pies and peach cobblers their

---

[18] Ibid., Vol. II, p. 150.
[19] The incident is recorded by Mrs. Victor in River of the West, p. 51. This occurred at Meek's first rendezvous, which no doubt was attended by Newell.

mothers had made."[20] The proprietors of the camp had saved a few dried beaver tails and a little flour for just such an occasion. These were rationed out at the rate of one tail to every seven men. The tails were minced, and together with a small amount of flour and moss, stewed in a kettle with three gallons of water until quite thick. "This constituted our meal many pronounced it a first rate dish and wished they had a little salt to season it.[21]

The next day the search for game proved as fruitless as before. On the morning following, one of the men went back down the trail to bring up his horse, which had become too weak to walk the day before. The horse was a favorite and the hunter hoped a day's rest would be sufficient for the horse to recuperate. When he found the poor animal, it was still too weak to move, so the old hunter shot it and carried the meat back to camp. "That was the first time I ever saw stake fried in water. The most of the company having left the camp early they did not hear of the death of poor old Rock till night . . . ."

The party was in a terrible condition. "The night was passed by many dreaming of good things to eat which the morning proved to be dreams. To give a true picture of our party this morning would excite pity for the hunters life."[22]

One of the men had brought a dog along who was a pet in the camp. With the party in such terrible condition, the cleanliness of the meat or the propriety of eating animals usually considered unfit for human consumption were only of secondary importance. Before long the conversation around the various fires centered on the advisability of picking the bones of the camp watch-dog. Finally the owner was approached and asked for the dog. "My God," said he, "do you want to kill old Gunner? Can't you wait till night?" Gunner appeared to understand the conversation and went from fire to fire, as it would appear, to find sympathy and protection. A sharp crack from a rifle soon followed and Gunner was no more. There was sorrow among the men and tears fell from the eyes of his owner, James Mortin. Many swore they would as soon eat a piece of a man as of the poor old faithful watch-dog of

---

[20] The <u>Weekly Oregonian</u>, May 1, 1861. (Hereafter cited <u>Oregonian</u>.)
Article written by Newell of Champoeg under the pen name of "Mountaineer."
[21] <u>Ibid</u>.
[22] <u>Ibid</u>.

the camp. Others wished that the stomach that received a bite of it would be struck with inflammation. That day an elk was brought into camp. Many curses were heaped upon the murderers of "old Gunner". Joe Meek read the above story in the <u>Oregonian</u> and wrote the following: "Sir, I have passed many hard times with "Mountaineer" I helped him eat old Rock and Mortin's dog,"[23] substantiating Newell's story.

Newell was employed by several different companies during his ten years in the trapping business. In his diary he mentions the men who were his superiors without reference to the company name. His first employers, William Sublette and Jackson, sold out in 1830 to Milton Sublette, Freab, Fitzpatrick, Gervais and James Bridger. In the spring of 1833. Newell says, "I left Mr. Fitzpatrick the 25th of January and joined Capt. Bonneville. . . . I left Capt. Bonneville and engaged to Messers Fontinelle and Drips."[24] He fails to mention how long he stayed with Captain Bonneville. Following his visit to Ohio he says, "I engaged to Messrs Bent at St. Vrain."[25] The Next summer he again hired out to Drips and Fontinelle, who are the last mentioned in the diary.

The 30th of March, 1838, William Newell was born. He was the second son born to Robert Newell and his Indian wife.

The later years of the 1830's were years of declining fur values. The trappers were no longer able to harvest the rich profits they had enjoyed in earlier years. Newell's diary indicates the discouraging times the trappers were enduring. "Times is getting hard all over this part of the country, beever scarce and low, all peltries on the decline." And again he says: "Commenced sales, and men who had been in the company [Drips and Fontinelle] a long time commenced leaving, owing to the company being so hard. Some run off, stole horses, traps and other articles of value."[26] The thirteenth of June, 1840, he wrote: "I went to the American rendezvous, Mr. Drips, Freab and Bridger from St. Louis with goods, but times were certainly hard, no beever and everything dull."[27]

[23] <u>Oregonian</u>, May 20, 1861.
[24] Newell Diary, 1829.
[25] <u>Ibid</u>.
[26] <u>Ibid</u>.
[27] <u>Ibid</u>.

With conditions in the fur trade so discouraging, Newell and Meek decided to give up trapping shortly after the 1840 rendezvous. Both had survived their ten years' trapping in good condition. Newell had gained ten years' experience in methods of getting along with his fellow men in difficult situations. The fur companies he had worked for were engaged in cutthroat competition with each other and with the British. When Newell was delegated to trade with the Indians in dangerous circumstances, he conducted himself in such a manner as to gain their confidence. Contact with them had familiarized him with their manner of life and mores. Among the Nez Perce Newell had gained life-long friends. He had won the daughter of a Nez Perce sub-chief for his wife, and she bore him four sons, Francis, William and Marcus Whitman Newell, in 1835, 1838, and 1840, respectively, and Robert Newell, Junior, after the family had settled in the Willamette Valley.

Sometime during his ten years in the mountains Newell acquired the title of "Doctor." In those days "Doctor" was bestowed with little thought or concern as to the educational background of the receiver. He had gained a knowledge of some simple remedies through the use of roots and herbs, which worked alike on "dogs, horses, Indians and his fellow Trappers," and was nicknamed "Doctor" because of his success.[28] The name stuck with him all his life and few took offense at the honor.[29]

Newell was no longer conspicuous for his youth or the holes in the "elbo" of his coat, but he was "full of humanity, good will, genial feeling, and frankness. He possessed a remarkable memory, and though slow of speech his narrations were most interesting.[30] Peter H. Burnett thus described him, adding a picture of his personal appearance: "He was of medium height, stout frame, and fine face."

The reckless life of the trappers with its attendant drunkenness and debauchery was a degrading experience for many of the participants, but there is reason to believe that Newell, if he took part at all in the revelry, did so with moderation. Not that he was a teetotaler or a wallflower, but ". . . his conduct was always

---

[28] Elliott, op. cit., p. 104

[29] W. H. Gray was one of the exceptions, as shown in his History of Oregon (Portland, Oregon: Harris and Holman, 1800).

[30] Burnett, op. cit.

marked by prudence and good sense."[31] When he and a small group of trappers decided to leave the mountains, Newell was possessed of more means than his companions, an indication that he had not squandered his earnings on alcohol and gambling. His companion, Joe Meek, admitted that he had graduated in some of the vices of camp life and had often become "very powerful drunk," but there are no references to Newell's ever having been in such a condition.

---

[31] Manuscript by Jesse Applegate giving his estimate of Newell, Bancroft Library. Caroline C. Dobbs said of Newell: "Although in camp life he was a leader and his jollity in song and story around the camp fire was long remembered, he never demeaned himself with debauchery which was so common at the rendezvous or lost the inherent instincts of a gentleman." See Caroline C. Dobbs, Men of Champoeg (Portland: Metropolitan Press, 1932). p. 151.

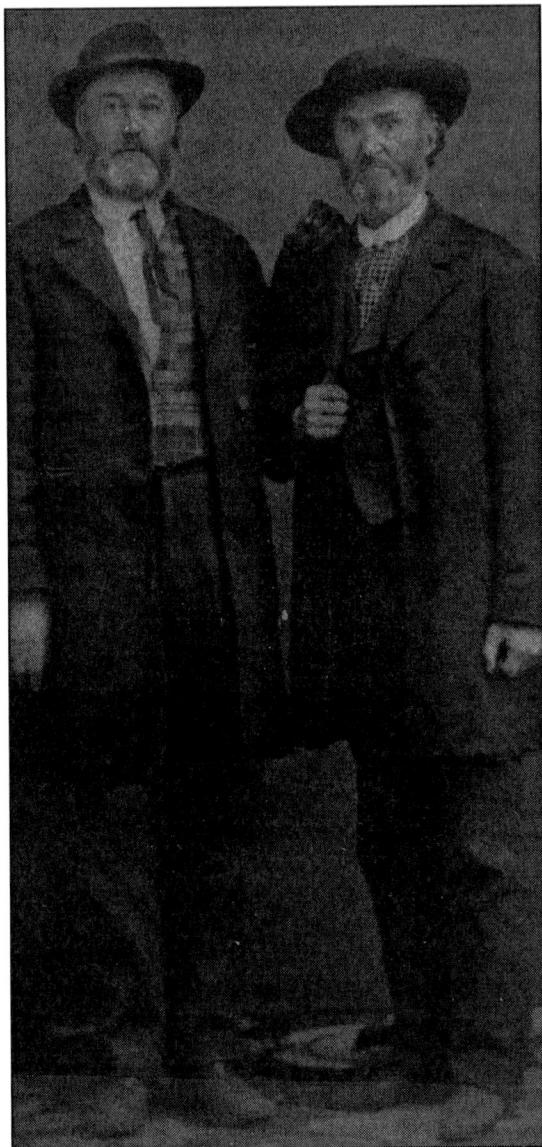

Joe Meek and Robert Newell, Trappers and Companions
Photo courtesy of the Champoeg State Heritage Area
Champoeg, Oregon

CHAPTER II

THE FIRST WAGONS IN OREGON

The withdrawal of the American fur companies from the mountains presented a serious problem to those men who had made a living by trapping, trading, and hunting. Newell and Meek were scarcely thirty years of age and were being cut off from their means of livelihood. Some of the men no doubt longed to return to the United States, to their relatives and friends. But their Indian wives and half-breed children would not make their reception in eastern communities easy. Some were too poor to return to their homes. Trappers were never famous for financial stability, and a change of occupation was inevitable.

One of Newell's fellow trappers, George W. Ebberts, left the mountains in 1838,[1] and about fifteen went down the Columbia in 1839. The Rev. John S. Griffin and Asahel Munger and their wives, missionaries present at Fort Hall in 1839, noted the sad condition of the trappers. In the Mungers' diary, they described conditions at the fort: "The scene we have left is really distressing. Those poor mountain men are receiving payment in alcohol at an enormous price. These men now scatter off . . . and seek a home and employment where they can. Many of them are so poor they cannot go down to the States—What to do they know not."[2]

One condition contributing to their departure was Indian hostility. Relations were poor partly because of the careless attitude of the less responsible trappers who stole horses from the Indians and in other ways were offensive. According to Indian law, if one offended, his whole tribe was held responsible. Thus the few careless trappers endangered the lives of their innocent companions.[3]

In February, 1840, Newell left "Brown's Hole . . . for Fort Hall," a trip he had made before in eleven days, but which, because

---

[1] Tobie, <u>No Man Like Joe</u>, p. 84
[2] Quoted by Tobie, <u>op. cit.</u>, p. 78
[3] Victor, <u>River of the West</u>, p. 259; "Journal of E. Willard Smith, "<u>O. H. Q.</u> (September, 1913), XIV:268; Newell Diary, 1829.

of the heavy snow at this time, required forty-five days.[4] At Fort Hall Newell met Joe Meek and the following conversation ensued:

"Come" said Newell to Meek. "We are done with this life in the mountains—done with wading in beaver dams, and freezing or starving alternately—done with Indian trading and Indian fighting. The fur trade is dead in the Rocky Mountains and it is no place for us now if it ever was. We are young yet and have life before us. We cannot waste it here; We cannot or will not return to the states. Let us go down to the Wallamet and take farms. There is already quite a settlement there made by the Methodist Mission and the Hudsons Bay Company's retired servants.

"I have had some talk with the Americans who have gone down there, and the talk is that the country is going to be settled up by our people, and that the Hudsons Bay Company are not going to rule this country much longer. What do you say Meek? Shall we turn American settlers?"

"I'll go where you do Newell. What suits you suits me."

"I thought you'd say so . . . In my way of thinking a white man is a little better than a Canadian Frenchman. I'll be d---d if I'll hang around a post of the Hudsons Bay Company. So you'll go?"

"I reckon I will! What have you got for me to do? I haven't got anything to begin with but a wife and baby."[5]

---

[4] Newell Diary, 1829. For the location and distances between these and other Forts see the map in Chittenden, op. cit., Vol. II

[5] Mrs. Victor, who interviewed Joe Meek, records the conversation, River of the West, pp. 264-5.

With their destination settled, the two hardened mountain men made preparations to go to the Willamette Valley. They were admirably fitted to take their places there, and were to play an important part in its development.

The manner in which Newell acquired the two wagons, which he took to Oregon, is an interesting one. While he was at the American rendezvous at Green River in June of 1840, some missionaries arrived bound for the Columbia River. "I engaged to pilot them over the mountains, with their wagons and such used in crossing to Fort Hall . . . . I had some difficulty with a man named Moses Harris. I think he intended murder. He shot at me about 70 or 80 yards but done no damage only to himself."[6] This incident was explained in more detail in 1867 when Newell described his argument with Harris[7] and his acquisition of the wagons.

The missionaries were "Rev. Harvey Clark (principal), Mr. Smith and Little John."[8] "They had no idea of the road or the country before them, were without a guide and with their wives and

---

[6] Newell Diary, 1829.

[7] In 1867 Newell was involved in a controversy with W. H. Gray relative to the early history of Oregon. William H. Gray was born in 1810 at Fairfield, New York. After coming to Oregon in 1836 he was identified with several different missionary projects. He was influential in the early provisional government and throughout his life in Oregon was prominent. His part in the formation of the early government and a critical account of his history will be found below. For his biography see Evans, History of the Pacific Northwest: Oregon and Washington (North Pacific History Company, 1889), Vol. II, pp. 348-50; Scott, History of the Oregon Country, 5 Vols. (Cambridge: Riverside Press, 1924), Vol. I, p. 159; Oregonian, November 15, 1889. One of the disputed facts related to Newell's wagon journey to the Willamette. Gray had held the Hudson's Bay Company responsible for discouraging the early immigrants from attempting to take their wagons beyond Fort Hall. Gray's account was published in the Astoria Marine Gazette—see George S. Turnbull, History of Oregon newspapers (Portland, Oregon: Binford and Mort, 1939), pp. 301-303. These articles were later published in Gray's History of Oregon, op. cit. Newell answered these articles in the Oregon Herald (see Turnbull, op. cit., pp. 150-152). He had received many inquiries as to the make-up of the party and wrote as nearly as he could remember, the incidents of the journey.

[8] Newell Diary, 1829.

two wagons, they looked upon their situation as rather critical."[9] Mr. Clark had made some sort of an agreement with Harris, known in the mountains as "Blackie" Harris. Mr. Clark discussed the matter with Newell, explaining that Harris had asked such a high price to guide them to Fort Hall that all their money would be needed to pay him. Newell understood the situation and agreed to guide them for much less.

> We went and saw Harris who was much dissapointed to find out that he had failed to extract the little money these poor men had . . . . On the next morning I got upon my horse and went back to bid adieu to old messmates and mountain companions and started off and had got about eighty yards when Harris who I had not seen that morning took a shot at me after remarking that I would not live to stand between him and another trade. The shot was close but a miss. I wheeled and galloped toward Harris who ran and hid in a thicket and was denounced by all in camp—and Capt. Dripps told him that had his ball struck me he would have hung him. None hardly in those days were disinclined towards the missionaries.[10]

After the group arrived at Fort Hall, Newell bought the wagons.[11] Mr. Smith, one of the missionaries, states: "One wagon and double harness we gave to Bob Newell to pay for piloting us from Green River to Fort Hall."[12]

The missionaries wished to continue their journey as soon as possible, but their horses were too worn out to go on to the Willamette without rest. To meet this situation, Newell exchanged

---

[9] Correspondence to the Herald. This correspondence between Newell and the editor of the Herald in Newell's own handwriting is preserved in the Oregon Historical Society in Portland. Hereafter cited MS 979.1.

[10] Ibid.

[11] Newell Diary, 1829. This diary states that he bought two wagons from the missionaries, and two from Joel Walker, which he sold to the Hudson's Bay Company.

[12] Quoted by Elwood Evans, op. cit., I:219. Evans quotes a letter written to him by Newell recounting his experiences as leader of the first wagon party to arrive in Oregon.

animals with Clark, and the missionaries packed their belongings on the fresh animals and set out on July 5, 1840.[13]

Newell and his mountain friends stayed at Fort Hall while the animals, which they had secured in trade recuperated. By September 27 they were ready to start.[14] Members of the party were Robert Newell, his Indian wife and three boys, Francis Newell, five, William Newell, two, and Marcus Whitman Newell, five months; Joe Meek, his wife and baby girl, Helen Mar; Caleb Wilkins, Mr. Craig, Mr. Larson, and a German called Nicholas. Newell found "None but Wilkins . . . willing to undertake the wagon experiment which was just what I wanted to do."[15]

Newell offered Francis Ermatinger, at that time in charge at Fort Hall for the Hudson's Bay Company, a wagon in return for a man and all the assistance he could give to make the experiment a success. Ermatinger was anxious to have a wagon road opened to Walla Walla and agreed to Newell's proposition. He". . . was quite liberal to us all . . . . Mr. Calib Wilkins bought a wagon of Joel Walker and was anxious to make the trial . . . . We made a start Wilkins driving his own team, Nicholas (a german) driving Mr. Ermatinger's and Mr. Meek driving the one belonging to myself."[16]

The party had not gone far when they began to realize the difficult task they had begun. It must have been a rough ride over lava beds, across mountains, through forests, fording rivers, and accompanied always by the crashing of sagebrush against the wagon bed. The animals used to pull the wagons began to fail rapidly and it became necessary to lighten their loads. They were finally forced to abandon the wagon boxes, and Newell said: "we were quite sorry that we had undertaken the job and all the consolation we had was that we broke the first sage on that road . . . ."[17]

---

[13] MS 979.1, Diary of A. T. Smith in the Historical Society, Portland, Oregon. Newell Diary, 1829.

[14] Newell's Diary of 1829 gives the date September 17, 1840, as the starting date. In 1867 he says the date was August 5th. I have used the date given in his diary, as it seems most likely to be correct.

[15] MS 979.1.

[16] Ibid. Elwood Evans included Ermatinger in the party but he was not with the group according to Newell's account. Evans, op. cit., p. 220. Also Transactions of the Oregon Pioneer Association 1877, p. 22 (hereafter cited O.P.A.T.).

[17] Ibid.

At Fort Boise, another Hudson's Bay post, the party stopped to rest a few days. With the usual courtesy of the company Mr. Payette, who was in charge of the fort, offered Newell, the leader of the party, quarters within the fort. He also sent a piece of sturgeon to those who were not invited to share company quarters. Such an emphasis on rank was anathema to the ardent republicanism of the frontiersmen. Though they were forced to live on dried salmon skins after their provisions were gone, the sturgeon was returned.[18]

After replenishing their supplies the party continued on to the Walla Walla Valley, where "In a rather rough and reduced state we arrived at Dr. Whitman's station or mission . . . ."[19] Dr. Whitman brightened the spirits of the tired, discouraged travelers by "feasting" the entire party. When he heard Newell mention his regrets at having undertaken to transport wagons to Oregon he said: "Ah, you will never regret it; you have broken the ice, and when others see that wagons have passed, they too will pass; and in a few years the valley will be full of our people."[20]

The reception must have impressed the mountain men, for Newell named his third son Marcus Whitman, and Joe Meek left his little half-breed daughter Helen Mar in the care of the Whitmans.[21]

The Indians were much amused by the wagons, which they called "horse canoes." They walked round and round the curiosities and then "seemed to give it up."[22]

The party enjoyed a day or two at the mission and then moved on to the Company post, Fort Walla Walla. Newell mentions especially the warm kindness with which they were

---

[18] Tobie, op. cit., pp. 85, 86. Victor, op. cit., pp. 279-80. MS 979.1.

[19] Evans, op. cit., p. 220. MS 979.1. Oregon Herald, March 3, 1867.

[20] Ibid. See also Clifford E. Drury, Marcus Whitman M. D. Pioneer and Martyr (Caldwell, Idaho: The Caxton Printers, 1937), pp. 238, 239. The mountain men had known the Whitmans before, having met them while the missionaries were traveling to Oregon. See River of the West, pp. 208-213.

[21] Mrs. Whitman later wrote that the child was fretful, stubborn, and difficult to manage and that her body was dirty, covered with lice and poorly clad. She later, to some degree, filled the aching void left by the loss of their own daughter who had drowned. See Drury, op. cit., p. 239. Mrs. Victor states that Meek's wife, "persisted in abandoning him in the mountains . . . . which would explain his decision to leave his little girl at the station.

[22] Evans, op. cit.; MS 979.1.

received. Here the party disbanded. Craig and Larison went to Spalding's mission at Lapwai,[23] while Newell, Meek, and families, with one Snake Indian whom Newell brought to Oregon, continued their journey on horseback. At that time the wagons were left at the fort. The following year one was taken down the Columbia River, which event Newell recorded as follows: "There I left one wagon, and the other I had took down in a boat to Vancouver . . . . This is to be remembered that I, Robert Newell was the first who brought wagons to Oregon across the Rocky Mountains."[24]

The little party arrived at The Dalles worn and tired, but the welcome, which awaited them, was not the kind-hearted greeting they had received at Waiilatpu and Fort Walla Walla. They arrived on Sunday and the missionaries in charge refused them food and lodging in an earnest attempt to keep the Sabbath holy. Newell said of the reception: "I never was treated so badly in my life by our Americans as we were at The Dalles."[25] They camped a few miles below the mission for the night. David Carter, who, with Jason Lee, was making an official visit to the mission to conduct a camp meeting, explained to the men the reason for the lack of hospitality and invited them to a prayer meeting being held that night. The hungry travelers were more interested in feeding their bodies, but the missionaries insisted that they feed their souls. They went to the meeting, as Newell says, "to show him that we could pray as well as fast."[26]

---

[23] Clifford M. Drury, Henry Harmon Spalding, (Caldwell, Idaho: The Caxton Printers, 1936), p. 259.

[24] Newell Diary, 1829. H. E. Tobic, op. cit., pp. 80-85, suggests that Newell left the mountains in a superior position to the other mountain men and the trip was possibly undertaken at the request of the Hudson's Bay Company. Since Newell rode a horse and did not drive a wagon, Tobie credits the drivers of the wagons for their trip. Newell was never in the employment of the Hudson's Bay Company. MS 979.1.

[25] MS 979.1. The mission was in charge of Daniel Lee and Mr. Perkins, Methodist Missionaries. Jason Lee was preaching to the Indians at The Dalles at this time. "Reminiscences of Daniel Lee," Microfilm in Oregon Historical Society.

[26] Ibid. Mrs. Victor gives an account of the meeting, which tells of Jandreau, a Frenchman, making a mock prayer with such earnestness and apparent genuiness that the missionaries joined him with loud amens and hallelujahs. The trappers could not control their laughter for the

Friendly Indians supplied them with dried salmon the next day and this became their principal food for weeks. As the little party made their way down the Columbia they were buffeted by wind and rain. Newell had brought two footsore cows from Green River and had been given a bull by Dr. Whitman at Waiilatpu. With these animals they crossed the Columbia to the north side. "Swimming our stock above the Cascades and at the mouth of the Sandy we recrossed the same way and made our way to the Willamette Falls."[27] The date of arrival was December 15, 1840, as recorded in Newell's diary.

There was no information center at which to inquire as to the best place to lodge. There were no hotels and no restaurants where they could obtain a hot meal. After traveling all day in the rain and mud with only dried salmon to eat and no place to stay except the usual camp, the hungry, dirty, tired trappers must have been discouraged as they busied themselves setting up a camp. They had arrived at last in the Willamette Valley, but the valley in 1840 was little more than a wilderness. Newell left this little note of disappointment, "This country is not so good as supposed."[28]

Frenchman was reciting one of the tales of the Arabian Nights, which they all knew. River of the West, pp. 281-283

[27] MS 979.1.

[28] Newell Diary, 1829.

CHAPTER III

FOUNDING THE PROVISIONAL GOVERNMENT

In the camp at the Falls Newell and Meek were joined by their old friends Dougherty, Wilkins, and Ebberts. All were seeking a place to settle.

It has been noted that Newell was in a superior position when he left the mountains. "Newell had the advantage over Meek in several particulars. He had rather more book-knowledge, more business experience and also more means. With these advantages he became a sort of "Booshway" among his old comrades who consented to follow his lead in the important movements about to be made ...."[1]

Newell crossed the Columbia again to obtain dried salmon from Fort Vancouver. The only other source of supplies for the trappers was the Methodist mission at Willamette Falls, where the Rev. Alvin F. Waller and Alanson Beers were carrying on missionary work among the Indians. Reluctantly the missionaries gave the trappers a few potatoes.[2] Food was a real problem at the time, for the buffalo so easily obtained in the mountains were not to be found in the Willamette Valley. Newell was known among the Hudson's Bay Company fur traders and found his credit good with Dr. McLoughlin at Fort Vancouver.[3] After twice receiving a rather cool reception at the hands of the American missionaries, first at The Dalles and then at Willamette Falls, it is not surprising to find Newell speaking in terms of highest praise for the assistance he received from the Company.

There is no record of the determining factors, which influenced the trappers to choose the Tualatin plains for their homes, but it was on land near the present site of Hillsboro that they built wigwam-type shelters. No doubt the absence of trees was an important factor, for it offered the possibility of farming without the

---

[1] Victor, River of the West, p. 285. Booshway was the title given to the leader of a trapping party, the one in charge. Ibid., p. 49.
[2] Bancroft, History of Oregon, I:243.
[3] Tobie, No Man Like Joe, p. 94.

necessity of clearing away the forest, which covered so much of the surrounding area.[4]

They were joined later by the independent missionaries whom Newell had guided from Green River to Fort Hall. In October, 1841, the little community included: the trappers, Newell and his family, Mr. and Mrs. Meek, Dougherty, Walker, Wilkins, Ebberts, and Larison; the missionaries, Griffin, Clark, Smith, and Littlejohn.[5]

This first winter proved to be a miserable one. Snow fell early and the continuous rains made life in the hastily constructed shelters disagreeable. While in the mountains, the trappers had been able to live in a wigwam-type shelter and remain relatively healthy. Now they were confronted with continuous rains, and even if they could keep the roofs from leaking the ground underneath became wet and soggy. Newell wrote in his diary, "the climate is not so healthy, I have had some sickness and also my family."

With the coming of spring, Newell, Dougherty, Wilkins, and Walker obtained some farming equipment and seed wheat from the Hudson's Bay Company and set out to farm the land they had claimed. The Company gave them the equipment with the understanding that it should be paid for at their earliest convenience. The wheat was to be returned following the harvest. Despite the Company's disapproval of American settlers in the area, McLoughlin did not allow them to starve. When the immigrants needed food and implements he usually managed to supply them.

Just how dependent they were on the British Company and the Methodist mission can be seen from the following entry which Newell wrote in April, 1841; "This country is under the influence of the Hudson's Bay Company, and the Methodist mission. The farmers get all their supplies from the two places, and also they are resorted to for advice in case of death, to settle their affairs. The latter however does the most of this as these people (are) the people's choice."[6]

---

[4] Ibid., p. 96.
[5] William M. Dougherty, Cyrus H. Walker, Caleb Wilkins, George W. Ebberts, and Larison, the German. I have been unable to find mention of the latter's first name. John S. Griffin, Alvin T. Smith, Harvey Clark, P. B. Littlejohn.
[6] Newell Diary, 1829.

The year 1842 is passed over by Newell with one short comment. The last entry in his diary reads: "1842 is past." For his subsequent activity we must rely on an occasional letter written by Newell and on records kept by others.

In the period after 1842 Newell reached the peak of his career as a farmer and legislator. He was unquestionably the leader of his class of men from the time he settled in the Willamette Valley, and in a few years he was leader of the legislative body, which governed Oregon.

The need for some form of government was very soon felt. In February 1841, the death of Ewing Young emphasized the lack of a civil authority, which could administer the estates of the deceased. Since Young's estate was the largest west of the Willamette, and he left no will or apparent heirs, the disposition of his estate posed a difficult problem.[7] The urgency of the situation was expressed in the immediate assembly of settlers following the funeral ceremonies, "for the purpose of appointing officers for the government of the community."[8]

Not all of those settled in the area agreed that a government was necessary. The Company, as a British concern, did not advocate a government, which would in any way favor the United States. The French Canadians, outnumbering the Americans until the immigration of 1843, "broke off almost to a man on the pretense that since they were the subjects of Queen Victoria and did not wish to forswear their country, they could not consistently enter into any measures that might prove prejudicial to her Majesty's government."[9] Another faction wanted to organize a government independent of all other nations. J. Quinn Thornton says that Chief Factor John McLoughlin favored such a government.[10] As late as 1844 there were those who advocated this solution.[11]

---

[7] Ewing Young, who arrived in November 1834, was the first American settler to claim land west of the Willamette River. He was a man of business acumen and soon became the wealthiest independent settler in Oregon. See Harvey W. Scott, History of the Oregon Country, I:298. II:6-7. For Government, see O.P.A.T., 1874, p. 52. See also Gustavus Hines, Wild Life in Oregon (New York: Worthington Co., 1881), p. 422.

[8] Hines, op. cit., p. 418.

[9] Ibid., p. 422.

[10] Thornton, op. cit., p. 59.

[11] The Spectator, first paper published in Oregon, printed an article on June 24, 1847, that mentions this early agitation for an independent government:

With allegiance almost equally divided and with conflicting ideas as to the most effective course it was necessary that those interested in securing a government primarily under the allegiance of the United States proceed cautiously.

The Falls Association, established in 1842 "for the mutual advancement of its members in discussion and composition . . . ."[12] discussed the possibilities of an independent government, but felt that such a government would be inexpedient "If the United States extends its jurisdiction over this country within the next four years."[13]

In addition to Ewing Young's death, an incident in the fall of 1842 served to quicken interest in a government. An Indian broke into the house of Rev. P. B. Littlejohn and carried away all that he could move. Some of Littlejohn's neighbors, the Rev. J. S. Griffin, Robert Newell, G. W. Ebberts, Caleb Wilkins, William Dougherty and Joe Meek, organized a vigilance committee, agreeing to assemble at the call of any of their group. An Indian was found who was familiar enough with the incident to make himself suspicious. When the committee questioned the Indian, he confessed his guilt. The judges deliberated on the matter and returned the sentence of "five lashes at the hands of each of the judges well laid on." The thief was bound to an oak tree and the lashes duly applied.[14]

The marauding wild animals, which killed the cattle of the settlers, gave rise to the so-called "Wolf Meetings." Even those who were not particularly interested in a governmental organization were concerned over the loss of their stock and sympathetic to any combined effort that would secure protection. The first of the Wolf

---

"In 1844 there were some of very respectable standing who advocated the idea of an independent form of government from an honest conviction doubtless that it was best calculated for the country in the isolated situation in which it was placed and the peculiar circumstances under which it existed . . . ."

[12] The Falls Association was the earliest literary and debating society in Oregon. Newell was one of the organizers. See Oregon Spectator, April 16, 1846; Marie Bradley, "Political Beginnings in Oregon," O.H.Q. (March, 1908), IX: 49; Charles H. Carey, A General History of Oregon Prior to 1861. 2 Vols. (Portland: Metropolitan Press, 1935), I:324-325; Trumble, op. cit., p. 25.

[13] Carey, op. cit., p. 325.

[14] Evans, op. cit., p. 234.

Meetings was held at the Oregon Institute on February 2, 1843. Little was accomplished save the appointment of a committee to notify the public that a general meeting would be held "at the house of Mr. Jos. Gervais on the first Monday in March next, at ten o'clock A.M. . . ."[15]

The second Wolf Meeting in March 1843, established bounties on wild animals and appointed a committee of twelve "to take into consideration the propriety of taking measures for the civil and military protection of this colony."[16] Robert Newell was a member of this committee and his name appears for the first time in Oregon's political history in the official minutes of the second Wolf Meeting.[17]

Another member of the committee was W. H. Gray, originally a secular member of the Whitman-Spaulding mission. Newell and Gray were active in the early Oregon Government for many years. No record of personal enmity between the two appeared until Gray published a series of articles in the Astoria Marine Gazette attacking Newell and other members of the early legislature. The two men were never reconciled, and wrote stinging criticisms of each other, both claiming the other could not be trusted. Perhaps the best point about the argument was the amount of material on early Oregon history that it brought out.

The committee of twelve selected by the second Wolf Meeting called a general assembly for May 2, 1843, a meeting, which some writers have claimed saved Oregon for the United States. Exactly what happened at the gathering never can be known for certain. The few accounts written at the time are contradictory or ambiguous, and subsequent accounts by participants seem to grind one axe or another. A detailed examination of the various

---

[15] LaFayette Grover, The Oregon Archives including the Journals, Governor's Messages and Public Papers of Oregon Asahel Bush, Public Printer, 1853, p. 8. (Hereafter cited Oregon Archives).

[16] Ibid., p. 11.

[17] Ibid. John Minto, who arrived in Oregon in 1844, wrote of these Wolf Meetings: "the founding of the provisional government of Oregon May 2, 1843, originated at a meeting called for an organization to destroy the wolves, bears and panthers which were the natural and very destructive enemies of settled life in Oregon in 1843." John Minto, "Hearing the Cry of the Wild," MS in his own handwriting at Oregon Historical Society. Minto left valuable comments on the political situation in the 1840's. See Bancroft, op. cit., I: 551; and Evans, op. cit., II:469-71.

accounts sheds some light at least on the activity of Newell in his position as leader of the mountain men.

The motley group of settlers who met at Champoeg on May 2, 1843, must have presented a colorful and picturesque sight.

> Every person was a law to himself as to the style of his dress. No white shirted persons—" biled rags" in the vernacular of the time were present. . . . The French settlers were clothed in Hudson's Bay Company stuffs, calico shirts, brown corduroy and moleskin pants with moccasins on their feet, with broad-brimmed black felt hats. Among them the scarlet silk sash with the long fringes was frequently worn instead of a belt. The mountain men, Americans were mainly dressed in buckskin suits with ample fringes and the same soft hats although no two were alike. The American settlers were clad in the residue of garments they had left over from crossing the plains . . . .[18]

Since the assembled persons differed in language and ideology as well as fashion, an easy agreement appeared hopeless. It is certain that there was considerable opposition present on that memorable May 2, but exactly where it lay, whether the division was completely along the lines of nationality, is still in doubt.

Two of the most complete accounts recorded by any of those who attended the meeting are by W. H. Gray and Robert Newell, both recorded at least twenty years after the event, and with certain lines of thought in mind. Up to the time of the meeting most of the American "settlers" in the Oregon country were the missionaries and their secular affiliates—except for the group of more or less independent trappers and mountain men led by Newell. The third general group consisted of the French-Canadians, for the most part retired employees of the Hudson's Bay Company. The Company itself was certainly not in favor of encouraging by any means the settlement of the area by Americans, though McLoughlin, as literal Company sovereign in the area, tempered the policy with humanity.

---

[18] George H. Himes, article in the Oregonian, May 3, 1901.

William H. Gray
Courtesy of Champoeg State Heritage Area,
Champoeg Oregon

Of the three groups, Gray represents an archtype of the secular end of the missionary or "mission party," as it was called. For most of this group, the Company and/or the Catholic priests represented the "tentacles of foreign monopoly" at their worst. This was Gray's axe, and he ground it to a stub.

It was Gray's claim, then, that those opposing the formation of a government were solidly French Canadian and led by the Hudson's Bay Company. His estimate of Dr. John McLoughlin was a paradox. McLoughlin as an American Gray admired as "noble" and "generous"; but in McLoughlin the representative of the Company, he could "at the same time . . . see the low debasing and mean spirit of the Englishmen as manifested in the attempt to deprive the American Republic of its rightful domain."[19]

Gray accused Newell of representing this same foreign interest.

> Perhaps the reader will understand Mr. Newell
> better if he is more fully informed as to his real
> genealogy, as there has always been a little doubt

---

[19] Gray, op. cit., p. 29.

whether he belongs to the American native or British Kingdom. From the best information we could get about him he was formerly from Cincinnati, Ohio and the Rocky Mountains. From the earliest history we have of him he has claimed to be an American and represented the interests of a foreign monopoly, under a religious belief that he was conscientiously right in so doing. By keeping himself talking strong American sentiments to Americans and acting strong anti-American while in the mountains and in the settlement he succeeded in obtaining and holding positions to benefit the trade of the Hudson's Bay Company; a place in the legislative committee and in the settlers government to shield and protect those who were seeking the destruction of all American trade and influence in the Company. He was at this time and has continued to be a faithful representative of the Hudson's Bay Company and Jesuit interests in the country for which service they should enter his name upon their calendar of saints. As a public man we are not aware that he ever originated a single act or law' but as representing a clique or the interest of his masters he has always been ready to do his utmost in every possible way.[20]

Newell never denied that he regarded the Hudson's Bay Company with esteem. He was impressed by the magnanimity of Dr. McLoughlin in his relations with the early settlers. He especially mentioned the assistance given Jedediah Smith after his furs had been stolen and his party nearly all murdered by the Indians.[21] Newell admitted his friendly relations with the Company. "Being in opposition to them for some years gave me an opportunity to learn something of their system and policy among the Indians and Americans. Though having been raised (and in fact educated) like most of my countrymen, prejudiced I changed my opinion as clever writers say men often do though a fool never." The superior methods and advantageous position gained by the Hudson's Bay

---

[20] Ibid., p. 342.
[21] MS 979.1

Company led Newell to advise the American Fur Company to withdraw from the trade west of the Rocky Mountains. "I advised it but am unable to say what influence it had but I know I lost a good situation . . . ."[22]

A careful examination of Newell's opinions as gleaned from his letters and his strictures on Gray proves conclusively that he was sympathetic to the Hudson's Bay Company; but there is no evidence that Newell ever championed the cause of the British Company when the interests of the United States were involved. It has been shown that Newell was received with indifference bordering on discourtesy by the Methodist missionaries in Oregon and that he was forced to seek aid from the Hudson's Bay Company who gladly extended him credit. He had no reason to feel obligated to the "mission party" which Gray represented.[23]

Gray's attempt to brand Newell a traitor to the United States seems based only on Gray's own opinion.[24] To the writer, the evidence indicates that Newell was strongly pro-American, though honest and sincere in his praise of the Hudson's Bay Company. There is no instance on record in which Newell advocated policies that were in any way preferential to a foreign country.

Newell and his neighbors, the mountain men, attended the meeting at Champoeg on May 2. The members of this group were

---

[22] MS 979.1. Gray recalled a remark Francis Ermatinger had made to him in 1837, which he used to show that Newell advised the American Fur Company to cease operations in the interest of the Hudson's Bay Company. "Mr. Ermatinger stated to W. H. Gray that Doctor Newell (as he was called) was worth more to the Hudson's Bay Company than any two of the best fur traders the company had." Gray had written this statement to the editor of the Oregon Herald who printed it. Newell felt an explanation was in order. He explained that he had never so much as asked for a position with the Company. For a completed discussion of the competition of the Fur Companies, see Chittendon, op. cit.

[23] Bancroft, op. cit., Vol. I, p. 126; Scott, op. cit., Vol. I, pp. 138, 159, Vol. V. pp. 234, 235.

[24] Gray's opinions were one of his strong points. He was an individualist who was not entirely popular within his own group. See H. H. Spalding to Greene, Oct. 15, 1842, Letters and Papers of the American Board of Commissioners for Foreign Missions, V:138; also Rev. Chauncey Eddy to David Greene, Feb. 17, 1836, cited in Clifford L. Drury, Henry Harmon Spalding (Caldwell, Idaho: 1936), p. 129.

. . . a distinct type, who got their name from their experiences hunting and trapping in the mountains. They were inured to hardship, rough and ready yet genial and hospitable. There was no malice in them. They never made mischief between neighbor and neighbor. But most of them were given to exaggeration when relating Rocky Mountain adventures. They seemed to claim the privilege of romance and fable when describing these scenes.[25]

According to Peter H. Burnett, Newell was one of two exceptions to the rule, and his "statements could be relied upon implicitly.[26]

T. C. Elliott said of these mountain men: "Reckless and illiterate? No! Squaw men in any odious sense of the word? No! Teetotalers? No! One hundred percent Americans? Yes!"[27] Not even Gray charged Newell or any of the mountain men with objecting to any governmental organization. He could charge Newell with hypocrisy, but Newell's activity among the pro-government forces was so obvious that even a man of Gray's mendacity dare not include Newell or the other mountain men with those who opposed organization.

At the appointed time the settlers assembled in the open air. Dr. Ira L. Babcock was chosen chairman, and Gray, Le Breton and Wilson secretaries.[28] George Le Breton was the only secretary who left any record of the meeting. His account is the most valuable source available though it contains a contradiction on the most controversial aspect of the meeting, the margin of victory in the vote to organize.

> The committee made their report, which was read and a motion was made that it be accepted, which was lost.

---

[25] Burnett, op. cit., p. 154. As an example of their exaggeration Burnett relates a story Joe Meek told him. Meek was out hunting by himself and his horse ran away from him. He also lost the lock from his gun so he was forced to walk three hundred and eighty-five miles without anything to eat but a thistle root and that physicked him. Ibid., p. 158.

[26] Ibid., p. 154.

[27] T. C. Elliott, "Doctor Robert Newell, Mountain Man," Oregon Voter, August 20, 1927.

[28] Oregon Archives, p. 14.

Considerable confusion existing in consequence.

It was moved by Mr. Le Breton, and seconded by Mr. Gray that the meeting divide preparatory to being counted; Those in favor of the objects of this meeting taking the right and those of a contrary mind taking the left, which being carried by acclamation and a great majority being found in favor of organization, the great part of the dissenters withdrew.[29]

Le Breton's minutes clearly show that there was opposition to the report of the committee—so much opposition that the first vote to accept the report of the committee was lost. After the motion to divide for the count had carried by acclamation, Le Breton said the motion was carried by a great majority. It would be interesting and most helpful to know just what was meant by the words, "great majority."

There are very few contemporary or near contemporary accounts of the meeting besides Le Breton's official minutes, and none of these mention the details. Immediately following the meeting of May 2, 1843, Rev. John S. Griffin wrote: "The inhabitants of lower Oregon have this day assembled to consider measures . . . deemed necessary for mutual protection and safety."[30] Nothing of importance but the date of the meeting is mentioned in this account. Lansford W. Hastings, who was "Dr. McLoughlin's agent and probably the only American who was in the confidence of McLoughlin,"[31] left a few words about the meeting. He mentioned a strong movement among the settlers to declare themselves independent "of all powers of the world."

In Hastings's New Description of Oregon and California, published in 1857, he declared that "Neither the officers of the Hudson's Bay Company, nor any person in the service of that company, took any part in this governmental organization nor did

---

[29] Ibid.
[30] Unpublished MS by John S. Griffin, Oregon Provisional government papers, Oregon Historical Society, No. 1711.
[31] J. Neilson Barry, The French Canadian Pioneers of the Willamette Valley (Portland, Oregon: n.p., 1933), p. 10.

many of the Canadians or half-breeds, who had formerly been engaged in the service of the company."[32] Hastings emphasized the independent attitude of the Hudson's Bay Company men, but his statement that "not many" of the Canadians took part implies that some did take an active part in the government.[33]

Dr. John McLoughlin, chief factor of the Hudson's Bay Company at the time of the meeting, wrote several different times about the formation of the government in Oregon. He does not give specific dates and probably wrote of the general movement to organize a government. In his report to the Governor and Committee of the Company, dated London, November 15, 1843, the following paragraph appears:

> The American population of the Willamette Valley had a political meeting last May and invited the Canadians to unite with them in organizing themselves into a community. The Canadians who are fully as many as the others told them they would positively take no part in their plans of organization and government. The American party with a few Englishmen who came by way of the states and some Foreigners formed themselves into a body. . .but so far I am happy to say everything is quiet.[34]

Dr. McLoughlin's report of July, 1844, indicated some progress made by those in favor of a government: "The American Citizens called on the Canadians to join them and organize a government for themselves and though the Canadians refused last

---

[32] Lansford W. Hastings, <u>A New Description of Oregon and California</u> (Cincinnati: Quaker City Publishing House, 1857), p. 61. These few remarks were first written by Hastings and printed in the <u>Saint Louis New Era</u> in 1843. The full text of his remarks may be found in the <u>O.H.Q.</u>, II (June, 1901), p. 202.

[33] Newell's account stressed the fact that some of the French took part in the formation of the government, but he did not mention the Canadians.

[34] E. E. Rich, E. E. Rich, <u>The Letters of John McLoughlin From Fort Vancouver to the Governor and Committee</u> (Toronto, Canada: The Champlain Society Publishers, 1943), Second Series, pp. 129, 130.

year, yet seeing the increasing number of the Americans[35] and that it would be impossible to maintain peace and order in the country without organizing themselves, the Canadians consented.[36]

His report of August 12, 1844, also emphasizes the reluctance of the Canadians to participate.[37] Dr. McLoughlin felt the meeting was of sufficient importance to mention to his superiors, but if he knew the details of the meeting he made no mention of them other than to emphasize the reluctance of the Canadians to affiliate themselves with the new government.

G. W. Hines was in Oregon at the time of the meeting, although not present at the meeting.[38] Nine years after the meeting he published a book entitled Wild Life in Oregon in which he included Le Breton's minutes with no further description of the details. Hines used the words "large majority" instead of "great," but the meaning is not significantly changed.

J. Quinn Thornton,[39] an arrival of 1846, wrote an account in his book Oregon and California, published in 1849. He gave the date March 6, 1843, as the time when the legislative committee of nine was appointed, but does not mention the meeting of May 2, 1843. He is obviously in error, for the legislative committee was appointed on May 2, 1843, at the same meeting, which voted to organize a government.[40] Thornton gives a later account in the Transactions of the Oregon Pioneers for 1873, which follows Gray so closely that it seems beyond doubt a paraphrase of Gray's account.

Gray himself wrote an account of the meeting in 1866, twenty-three years after the meeting, with much more embellishment:

> The Hudson's Bay Company had drilled and trained
> their voters for the occasion under the Rev. F. H.
> Blanchet and his priests and they were promptly on

---

[35] For a description of the immigration of 1843 see Carey, op. cit., pp. 360-400. Political significance, p. 391. Also Frederic V. Homan, "Oregon Provisional Government," O.H.Q. (June, 1912), XIII:89-139.

[36] E. E. Rich, op. cit., p. 199.

[37] Ibid., Series 3, P. 4.

[38] Hines, op. cit., p. 154. Hines was on a journey to the interior on May 2, 1843.

[39] For his biography see Oregonian, February 4, 1888, p. 1.

[40] Oregon Archives, pp. 14, 15.

the ground in the open field near a small house, and to the amusement of every American present, trained to vote "No" to every motion put; no matter if to carry their point they should have voted "yes" it was "No." Le Breton had informed the committee and the Americans generally, that this would be the course pursued, according to instructions hence our motions were made to test their knowledge of what they were doing, and we found just what we expected was the case. The Priest was not prepared for our manner of meeting them, and as the record shows, "considerable confusion existing in consequence." By this time we had counted votes. Says Le Breton, "We can risk it; let us divide and count." "I second that motion" says Gray. "Who's for a divide?" sang out old Joe Meek as he stepped out; "all for the report of the committee and an organization, follow me." This was so sudden and unexpected that the priest and his voters did not know what to do, but every American was soon in line. Le Breton and Gray passed the line and counted fifty-two Americans and but fifty French and Hudson's Bay Company men. They announced the count—"Fifty-two for and fifty against." "Three cheers for our side," sang out old Joe Meek. Not one of those old veteran mountain voices were lacking in that shout for liberty. They were given with a will and in a few seconds the chairman, Judge I. L. Babcock, called the meeting to order, when the priests and his band slunk away into the corners of the fences, and in a short time mounted their horses and left.[41]

Gray follows this account with a copy of Le Breton's minutes, exact except for one important word. Where Le Breton had used "a great majority," Gray uses the word "majority," and his version of the official minutes reads: "A majority being found in favor of organization, the great part of the dissenters withdrew."[42] If

---

[41] Gray, op. cit., p. 279.
[42] Ibid., p. 280.

Gray were to harmonize his version with the official minutes it was necessary that the minutes be changed and it was a very simple task to remove one word without which the two accounts would agree, for a majority could mean fifty-two to fifty or fifty-one- to fifty, but a "great majority" just wouldn't fit.

In Gray's 1866 account there are other new elements: the exact number voting—one hundred and two; the organized priests leading the French-Canadians drilled by the Hudson's Bay Company in voting "No" on all motions; the exact number voting affirmatively with only two votes deciding the issue, and Joe Meek's dramatic call of "who's for a divide?"

Most secondary authors seem to have used Gray's added incidents as the very heart of their description of the May 2 meeting. Very few accounts do not include the fifty-two fifty vote or leave out Joe Meek's dramatic action. Yet these incidents were introduced twenty-three years after the meeting by a historian whom fair-minded critics have shown to be unreliable.[43]

When Newell read Gray's version of the meeting, he took up his pen and wrote an account of the meeting which was published in the <u>Oregon Herald</u> of December 9, 1866:

> The meeting was called to order and Doctor Babcock was elected President, and other officers of the meeting selected.
>
> A motion was then made that the convention proceed to organize a political government for the country, to continue and be in force until such times as the Government of the United States should establish a provisional government over the territory.
>
> The chairman put the question, and found the vote so close that he was unable to decide. He put the

---

[43] For criticism of Gray's writings by his contemporaries see Burnett, op. cit.; Waldo Critiques, MS 323, and Tolmie, Puget Sound, MS 24-25, Oregon Historical Society; in the Bancroft Collection: Moss, Pioneer Times, MS 16-17; Crawford, Missionaries, MS 3; White, Early Government, MS 40. Also in writings of Evans, Elliott, Victor, Blanchet and Applegate.

question again, saying, "Gentlemen, I am unable to decide. Those favoring the motion to organize will please say aye those opposed say no."

Again the chairman was unable to decide. A division was called for and the chairman said, "Those favoring the motion will form a line on the right. Those opposed on the left." (The meeting was held in the open air.)

As the two lines were being formed considerable pulling and hauling with sharp words, took place. After about half an hour the two lines were formed and tellers were appointed. The motion prevailed by five majority, but had the Frenchmen opposed the motion as W. H Gray says they did the motion would have been lost.

Having taken an active part in the affirmative, I recollect the names of some of the French who voted with us; and here they are, Jarvis (Gervais), Lucier, Billeque, Berbier, Ladaroot, Donpier and others.[44]

Newell disagreed with Gray's statement that the French were unanimously opposed to the government. He does not mention the total number of voters, but gives five as the winning majority. The conspicuous activity of Joe Meek is not mentioned. In direct contradiction to Gray, Newell ascribes to the French the honor of saving the day. Two new items are introduced. The "pulling and hauling" while the lines were forming and the elapse of one-half hour before the lines were formed.

The last account given by a participant was that of F.X. Matthieu, a pioneer of 1842. Matthieu was interviewed by Horace S. Lyman in 1900, when the old pioneer was eighty-two years of

---

[44] Robert Newell's account of the Champoeg meeting May 2, 1843. Ms 448, Oregon Historical Society. Also Oregon Herald, December 9, 1866.

age, fifty-seven years after the meeting. In Lyman's History of Oregon,[45] the interview with Matthieu is given in full:

> At the critical juncture however, after there had been some discussion and the meeting was becoming confused and indeed was in danger of breaking up without action, he remembers well how old Joe Meek strode forth and by the simple power of voice and example gained control after parliamentary tactics had failed. He cried out as he would to a company of militiamen, "All in favor of organization come to the right." One hundred and two were present. Fifty of these quickly went over to the right in favor of independence. The other fifty-two, all Canadians, remained as they were, or withdrew in the other direction . . . . His "mind was made up" he says, "ever since I left Canada. I knew what it was to live and die a slave under British rule." He said therefore to the Canadians that he was going with the Americans. He knew what he was doing and was fully decided which was the right side. Old Lucier, the trapper, followed him and now the vote stood fifty-two for and fifty against organization. Then went up the shout led by Joe Meek and his mountain men.[46]

Matthieu in the main substantiates Gray's account as to the closeness of the vote and Joe Meek's part, but takes credit for having influenced Etienne Lucier to vote with him—the deciding factor for victory.

Matthieu remembered too well that Gustavus Hines was present at the meeting, while Hines' journal clearly states that he was not present.[47]

---

[45] Horace S. Lyman, History of Oregon the Growth of an American State, 4 Vols. (New York: North Pacific Publishing Society, 19003), III:298-305.

[46] H. S. Lyman, "Reminiscences of F. X. Matthieu," O.H.Q. (March, 1900), I:94.

[47] Matthieu with the assistance of George H. Hines prepared a list of the names of those who voted affirmatively. Lyman, History of Oregon, p. 302. The validity of this list has been questioned. See J. Neilson Barry,

What are the conclusions to be drawn from these accounts? Only four of the accounts are contemporary. By far the most important of these is Le Breton's official record, and it does not mention the nationality of the opposition, and gives the winning margin as "a great majority" with no mention of Joe Meek.

J. S. Griffin left only a few words mentioning only the date and purpose of the meeting.

L. W. Hastings said very little about the meeting, but his statement that the Canadians broke off almost to a man with only a few taking part indicates that not all of the Canadians were opposed.

Dr. McLoughlin mentions a meeting in May of 1843, but his emphasis was on the unwillingness of the Canadians to be a part of a non-British government. No doubt he felt that such an emphasis was necessary in writing to his superiors. He mentions a "few foreigners" who took part in the government. Possibly he meant French or French-Canadians but his exact meaning cannot now be known for certain.

G. W. Hines, nine years after the meeting, follows Le Breton's minutes changing "great majority" to "large majority."

J. Quinn Thornton fails to mention the May 2 meeting until 1873 when he obviously follows Gray's account.

Of the controversial incident introduced by Gray, his statement that the French voted unanimously against the Americans has no corroboration whatever. Dr. McLoughlin's "few Foreigners" could have meant the French. Robert Newell names five French who voted with the Americans. Matthieu's account must be read cautiously because of his age at the time he described the meeting, but he says definitely that he and Lucier voted with the Americans.

Another of the men Newell says voted with the Americans was Joseph Gervais, whose home served as a center for the second wolf meeting. Both Gervais and Lucier were members of the committee of twelve then appointed to consider governmental possibilities. Gray stated that he and Le Breton had personally determined the opinion of all those appointed to this committee, that they "knew the feelings of the committee and there was not a

---

The French Canadian Pioneers of the Willamette Valley (Portland, Oregon: n.p., 1933). It seems rather remarkable that a man eighty-two years of age could recall the names of 52 people who voted affirmatively.

dissenting vote in that meeting."[48] It would seem logical to assume upon Gray's own authority that Lucier and Gervais were in favor of the governmental organization advocated by the committee of which Gray, Lucier, Gervais and Newell were members.

Gervais' political activity of the period is more proof that he was American in sentiment. In 1836 he signed a petition requesting the United States to take over Oregon. He was elected constable at the first wolf meeting and served from February 18, 1841, to July 5, 1843. In addition, he paid the voluntary assessment of 1844, and he ran for the legislature in 1845.[49]

The importance of Joe Meek at the meeting has been described many times. His latest biographer, H. E. Tobie, writes as Meek might have told it:

> Leaping to the front as he would have done to attach a clawing bear or clutching Indian, he shouted so that all could hear and understand, "who's for a divide . . . ." By a single, impulsive dramatic act an ex-mountaineer who could not fit into the new life of the settlements even as well as could his neighbors, the poor, ill-clad, unemployed clown rose to political leadership in Oregon. Immediately he was given not the easiest or most remunerative job in the new organization but an executive office, the most important office of all no doubt, that of sheriff.[50]

---

[48] Gray, op. cit., p. 267. For a complete refutation of Gray's 52-50 count see Charles B. Moore's "Pioneer Pot Pourri," O.H.Q. (December, 1926), XXVII:392.

[49] "The part of Joseph Gervais at Champoeg," Unpublished MS in the Oregon Historical Society. Bancroft has a MS from J. L. Parrish which admits Latourette (Laderoute) voted for the government, Russell B. Thomas, "Truth and Fiction of the Champoeg Meeting," O.H.Q. (September, 1929), XXX:235.

[50] Tobie, op. cit., p. 106. Bancroft, after describing Meek's call for a divide, cites Burnett's statement that Meek wore a "rich vest of white silk while the remainder of his clothing was exceedingly shabby." Burnett did not arrive in Oregon until November 25, 1843, and was not referring to Meek's attire on May 2, 1843, but Tobie describes Meek's appearance on May 2, 1843, as follows: "Clad in tattered clothing except for a fancy vest . . . ." Thus are errors perpetuated in history. Tobie has done an excellent

No one wishes to deny the redoubtable Joe Meek all the glory he deserves—anyone at all familiar with his life and character will admit that such a spontaneous reaction sounds very much like Joe. The great importance placed upon the episode since Gray's account was first published rests entirely upon his authority and the memory of Matthieu, who had probably read Gray's version many times before giving his description of the meeting in 1900. None of the other accounts so much as mention Joe Meek beyond his election as sheriff. The original provisional and territorial papers on file at the Historical Society in Portland do not mention any such incident.[51]

Joe Meek and Robert Newell were close friends until Newell's death in 1869. Something of their close relationship in the mountains has been discussed above. Newell fails to mention the important call. It seems most likely that Newell at least would have mentioned his friend's name if he had saved the day on May 2, 1843.

One fact can be stated without fear of successful contradiction. Meek's activity was not considered important at the time of the meeting. Not until 1866 was it mentioned, and after that date it was written and rewritten with dramatic effectiveness.

It is a still more difficult task to harmonize the various versions of the majority who voted in the affirmative. Le Breton's "great majority" would imply more than Newell's "five." and both discredit the fifty-two to fifty account of Gray and Matthieu.

Gray deliberately blackened the characters of those whom he opposed, and Newell was given many companions. For example, Robert Moore defeated Gray for the position of chairman of the legislative committee, which met on May 16, 1844.[52] Some of the

---

piece of work in combining historicity with readability which all will appreciate who read his work. What Meek wore is insignificant. The author is not seeking to tear down what has been done but is only illustrating how Meek's part has been emphasized. Victor's River of the West likewise ascribes to Meek an important part in the meeting, p. 321.

[51] Provisional and Territorial Papers of Oregon, No. 12186, in Oregon Historical Society. (Hereafter cited P. and T. Papers.)

[52] Newell read Gray's description of Moore and immediately explained to the public through the Oregon Herald that Gray and Moore were both nominated for chairman at the meeting of May 16, 1844. Newell evidently held Moore in high regard, for he came to his defense with the following:

petty prejudice, which animated Gray's writing, appears in his description of Moore:

> We will enter this hall and introduce you to an old grey headed man with fair complexion, bald head, light eyes, full face, frequent spasmodic nodding forward of the head and a large amount of self importance, not very large intellectual developments, with a super abundance of flesh and a good appetite to keep it above ordinary business necessities.[53]

Gray's attack on the Hudson's Bay Company becomes more understandable when one remembers the constant irritant of the long, drawn-out legal case in the sixties between the Company (its subsidiary, the Puget Sound Agricultural Company) and the federal government, especially to those of anti-British leanings. Then too, in 1866 Gray was employed by the United States government as revenue officer in Astoria, and it is possible that Gray felt it his duty to discredit the Company in order to damage its claims.

Gray was one of the first to publish a history of Oregon, and this partly accounts for his use as a primary source. But those who use his book must beware of his very plain prejudices in interpreting his "facts." Those who prefer a biased account with an emphasis on dramatization will find Gray's work most interesting.[54] The controversies precipitated by Newell's answers to Gray's history in many cases can only be decided individually. The majority of those who have made a study of the issues tend to accept Newell's statements as true. Russell B. Thomas, who seems especially impartial in his discussion of the Champoeg meeting, declares that "Newell's account was intended to correct certain misstatements

---

"Gray you were not worthy to rub tallow on old Bobby's shoes . . . . A good citizen, a patriot . . . and now that he is in his grave you propose to put him in your history as an unfair man as a set off to your vile slanders of the dead." MS 979.1

[53] Gray, op. cit., p. 336.

[54] Bancroft evaluates Gray's writing: "As a book of reference when compared to other authorities the work is valuable containing many facts and important documents. It has however three faults: lack of arrangement, acrimonious partisanship and disregard of truth . . . ." See op. cit., p. 302.

and false conclusions of Gray's and is probably correct. Gray does not at any rate refute him and really seems to acknowledge his corrections."[55]

J. Neilson Barry accuses Gray of being the lone falsifier in reporting the events of the meeting. "It made an interesting study although fictitious."[56] Such are the errors, which are too often perpetuated from the writing of a man of Gray's character. It makes a good story, but too often fits a pattern designed by the prejudices of its author.

One fact stands preeminently above the controversial issues. No matter how many voted affirmatively, and regardless of the nationality of the opposition, the vote to organize carried and a government primarily loyal to the United States was established.

It is a difficult task to judge accurately the real significance of the meeting. To place the responsibility of saving Oregon for the United States on the shoulders of Joe Meek or on the final outcome of the meeting is unquestionably an exaggeration. After 1825 Britain was willing to concede all land south of the Columbia River. In a document written in the handwriting of Dr. John McLoughlin there is valuable information as to the extent of the British claims: "Many of the Canadians objected to go to the Willamette because it was to become American territory, which I told them it would as the Hudson's Bay Company in 1825 officially informed that on no event could the British Government claim extend south of the Columbia."[57]

Great Britain and the United States were joint occupants of the Oregon Country at the time, and for Congress or the President to extend control over any part of the area in 1843 would have been a flagrant violation of the treaty. The area "on the northwest coast of America, westward of the Stony Mountains, shall, together with it's harbours, bays and creeks, and the navigation of all rivers within the

---

[55] Thomas, op. cit., p. 235.

[56] Unpublished article on "The Provisional Government" by J. Neilson Barry in Oregon Historical Society. Barry endeavors to show that Gray deliberately mixed the events of the meeting of March 4, 1844, with the May 2, 1843, meeting. "Some features of one mixed with some features of the other yet reversing." Barry's writing is at times ambiguous, confusing, and without proper documentation in this article. He has done exhaustive research on the subject and has written much valuable material. See his many articles in the O.H.Q.

[57] O.P.A.T. 1880, p. 46.

same be free and open, for the term of ten years from the date of the signature of the present convention, to the vessels, citizens and subjects of the two Powers . . . .'[58] Under such conditions Oregon "did not need savers—it was in no peril."[59]

The influx of American immigrants beginning with the immigration of 1843 made any settlement with Great Britain in which Britain acquired territory south of the Columbia most unlikely.

The formation of a provisional government gave the United States a foothold in the area, which the Hudson's Bay Company had dominated. The final settlement of the Oregon question was perhaps facilitated by this government, but again the preponderance of American settlers was no doubt more important than the governmental organization established in 1843. It signified a break in the Hudson's Bay Company's fur trading regime but even that was sure to come. The meeting of July 5, 1843, was more important in point of actual legislation passed, but the May 2 meeting was a beginning. And because it was the first meeting, which definitely decided to organize, it provided a foundation upon which the rest of the provisional government could grow, and functioned with efficiency quite remarkable considering the handicaps under which it existed.

> It will ever be one of the bright places in Oregon history to find that in spite of antagonizing jealousies and mutual distrust, a spirit of conciliation and compromise prevailed to bring together all the residents of Oregon territory, British and American citizens with the French-Canadians, people of diverse religions and unlike temperaments into a peaceful union for the purpose of maintaining a government having for its objects the protection of life and property.[60]

---

[58] Treaties and Conventions Concluded Between The United State of America and other Powers Since July 4, 1776 (Washington, D.C.: Government Printing Office, 1889), p. 416 (Hereafter cited Treaties and Conventions).

[59] Frederick V. Holman, "Oregon Provisional Government," O.H.Q. (June, 1912), XIII:120.

[60] Robert C. Clarke, History of the Willamette Valley Oregon (Chicago: S. I. Clarke Publishing Co., 1927), p. 305.

Newell's influence at the May 2 meeting has received very little attention. The popularization of Joe Meek has focused attention on "Old Joe" without proper evaluation of his associates, some of who were more influential. To date nothing has been found that would indicate that Newell played a conspicuous part in the meeting. The only place his name appears is in the list of the nine legislators appointed, but his activity in the legislature until 1849 is so outstanding that he was unquestionably the leader not only of the mountain men but of many others.

Jesse Applegate said that Newell "was the unquestioned leader of his class both British and American."[61]

F. X. Matthieu, another who knew Newell, paid tribute to his ability: "Newell was head and shoulders above all the other mountain men in his knowledge of government and in the knowledge of the methods necessary to be employed in organizing a government; in fact he was something of a statesman."[62]

"Every historian knows the ease of exaggeration by Joseph Meek. Newell and Meek were trappers in the mountains together in 1829, had shared life's escapes and privations and were life long friends but Newell was the deciding mind of the two as well as some of the Canadian settlers."[63]

Considering that Newell's background seemed to fit him for little more than fighting Indians and trapping beaver, it is quite remarkable, indeed it signifies unusual ability, to find Newell one of our early legislative leaders.

---

[61] Oregon Voter, August 20, 1927.

[62] Elliot, op. cit., p. 108.

[63] Oregon Voter, August 20, 1927.

CHAPTER IV

LIFE IN OREGON 1843-1847

There were other important measures agreed upon May 2, 1843, which influenced the early provisional government. Typical of the American frontier spirit was a strong feeling for personal liberty and a jealous regard as to the recipient of the executive authority. The first motion passed at the meeting after the vote to organize had carried was a motion, which stated that there should be no governor. Newell left an illuminating remark on this intense feeling of personal equality. "Dr. Babcock was a good man and wanted to be governor as did nearly all the rest so we had none."[1] This problem of where to place the executive authority caused some difficulty, but finally it was agreed that there should be a committee of three to act as the executive. Despite the compromise, Gustavus Hines felt that the triple executive was a "hydra headed monster in the shape of an Executive Committee which was but a repetition of the Roman Triumvirate—the Caesars upon the throne."[2]

It was at last decided that a committee of nine known as the legislative committee should be elected to prepare a plan of government to be submitted to the people on July 5, 1843. The committee consisted of "Messrs. Hill, Shortess, Newell, Beers, Hubbard, Gray, O'Neil, Moore and Dougherty."[3] It was moved and carried that these men receive for their services $1.25 per day with the privilege of convening a maximum of six days. The necessity of paying the legislators brought up the question of taxation – and

---

[1] Newell left some annotations in a copy of Grover's Oregon Archives. The original is in the Bancroft Collection; a microfilm copy is in possession of the author. These notes were obviously written after Newell's controversy with Gray for they note the time sequence at which the events of the argument transpired. There are a few valuable observations but most are written to censor Gray and are of little value.

[2] J. Q. Thornton, "History of The Provisional Government," O.P.A.T. 1874, p. 64.

[3] Oregon Archives, p. 15.

frontier pockets were tender. According to Newell the second motion passed was that no law should be passed to levy a tax.[4]

This first legislative committee had a great responsibility placed upon it. Possessed of little acquaintance with law-making and for the most part consisting of men of meager educational background, the committee was asked to produce a form of government which would satisfy the resident settlers in a maximum of six days. Though unlearned and unskilled in the finer arts of government, the committee worked for the best interest of the little community and pursued its objectives with honesty and sincerity. The result was a government admittedly not free of mistakes, as the frequent changes indicate, but one which, though "framed under such peculiar circumstances, gave the new country order, peace and security for six years."[5]

The legislative committee met in a building belonging to the Methodist mission and located "about eight miles below Salem."[6] In the first session on May 16, 1843, Robert Moore was elected chairman. Gray, Newell, and Shortess were appointed "to prepare rules and business for this house."[7] The report of the rules committee was adopted and the following committees appointed: judiciary, ways and means, military affairs, land claims, and county district divisions. These committees presented their reports throughout the remaining five meeting days on the 17th, 18th and 19th of May and on the 17th and 18th of June. By the 5th of July the legislature was prepared to report to the people of the territory.[8]

At Champoeg again "The inhabitants of Oregon Territory met, pursuant to adjournment, to hear the report of the legislative committee, and to do such other business as might come before them."[9] A committee was selected to draft an oath, which was

---

[4] The official minutes do not mention this vote although they say that the $1.25 per day for legislative members is to be raised by subscription. Oregon Archives, p. 15.

[5] Walter C. Woodward, The Rise and Early History of Political Parties in Oregon 1843-1868 (Portland, Oregon: J. K. Gill Company, 1913), p. 19.

[6] MS 979.1.

[7] Oregon Archives, p. 16. The importance of W. H. Gray in this legislative meeting is admitted even by Newell, although Newell presents Gray's activity with sarcastic digs at Gray. It is evident that Gray was an important member of this first legislature. See MS 979.1.

[8] Oregon Archives, pp. 16-22.

[9] Ibid., p. 23.

administered to the officers elected May 3, 1843. The legislative committee then made its report. The preamble emphasized the strong American influence present:

> We the people of Oregon Territory, for the purposed mutual protection, and to secure peace and prosperity among ourselves, agree to adopt the following laws and regulations until such time as the United States of America extend their jurisdiction over us.[10]

The division of the territory for executive purposes was accomplished by the creation of four districts. Twality comprised "all the country south of the northern boundary of the United States, west of the Willamette, or Multnomah River, north of the Yamhill River and east of the Pacific Ocean." Yamhill included "all the country west of the Willamette, or Multnomah River and a supposed line running north and south from said river, south of the Yamhill River to the parallel of 42° north latitude . . . and east of the Pacific Ocean." The third district, called Champooick, was "bounded on the north by a supposed line drawn from the mouth of the Anchiyoke River, running due east to the Rocky Mountains, west by the Willamette, or Multnomah River and a supposed line running due south from said river to parallel 42° north latitude; south by the boundary line of the United States and California and east by the summit of the Rocky Mountains." Clackamas, the fourth district, "comprehended all the territory not included in the other three districts."[11]

A bill of rights provided for freedom of worship; the right of habeas corpus and trial by jury with judicial proceedings "according to the course of common law"; all fines were to be moderate with no cruel or unusual forms of punishment. No laws were to be made to interfere or affect private contracts. Religion, morality and knowledge were to be encouraged through

---

[10] Ibid., p. 28.
[11] Ibid., p. 26.

maintenance of schools. The utmost good faith was to be observed toward the Indians and slavery was prohibited.[12]

The expenses of the government were to be raised by subscription. The subscribers pledged themselves "to pay annually, to the treasure of Oregon Territory the sum affixed to our respective names."[13]

The vote was limited to "Every free male descendent of a white man, an inhabitant of this territory of the age of twenty-one years and upwards."[14]

The organic law was in the main patterned after the Ordinance of 1787.[15] The laws of Iowa Territory were specifically named as those regulating "civil, military, and criminal cases; where not otherwise provided for and where no statute of Iowa Territory applies, the principles of common law and equity shall govern."[16]

The first laws proved so inadequate that the editor of the Spectator remarked in the issue of June 24, 1847: "We scarcely deem it worth while to give an abstract of the laws which were reported by the Legislative Committee and adopted by the people (July 5th) . . . as they were subsequently amended and perfected." They offer an interesting study, for they were produced by men of intense republican idealogy, but with little knowledge of jurisprudence. They show a determination to make a government, which was to be strictly a government by the people.

The immigration of 1843 considerably enlarged the community to be governed and emphasized the inadequacy of the laws passed. The government possessed no buildings; meetings were held in buildings of private citizens or those belonging to the mission. Voluntary subscription was not an adequate solution to the problem of the revenue needed for enlarged governmental responsibilities. Some felt that these glaring weaknesses were safeguards preventing the establishment of a state independent of the United States.[17] At the time the question of independence was

---

[12] Ibid., pp. 28, 29. Also J. Henry Brown, Political History of Oregon (Portland, Oregon: Wiley B. Allen, press of the Lewis and Dryden Printing Co., 1892), pp. 100, 101.

[13] Oregon Archives, p. 27.

[14] Ibid., p. 29.

[15] Woodward, op. cit., p. 22. Oregon Archives, pp. 30, 31.

[16] Spectator, June 24, 1847.

[17] Marie Bradley, "Political Beginnings in Oregon," O.H.Q. (March, 1908), IX: 54.

an important issue and Newell accused Gray of advocating an independent state in a speech in the legislature. Mr. Gray ". . . moved that the house go into the committee of the whole on the State of the Union and take into consideration the propriety of declaring ourselves independent of the Government of the United States."[18] It will be remembered that at the time of the organization of the government there was strong movement for independence. A sharp division developed between the old settlers and the new. Some of the settlers had brought slaves and objected to the ban prohibiting them. Some objected to government by an executive committee.[19] Under such conditions it is not surprising to find a new element in the government following the elections of May 1844. The legislative committee elected this year was the first law-making body named by election in Oregon. The 1844 legislature was composed of new men with the exception of two, David Hill and Robert Newell.

The legislative committee met on June 18, 1844, at the home of Mr. Hathaway.[20] M. M. McCarver was elected speaker. The same committees as those of 1843 were organized, with the exception of the committee on county districts, which was no longer needed. Newell was a member of the committee on Ways and Means and chairman of the committee on Land Claims. He was also appointed on a special committee to consider "a petition from J. L. Parish for the establishment of an additional district at Clatsop."[21] Dr. John McLoughlin asked for permission to construct a canal at the Willamette Falls and this was referred to another special committee of which Newell was a member.[22]

Liquor plus Indians was a combination feared by many of the settlers, and a bill "for the prevention of the introduction, sale and manufacture of ardent spirits in Oregon" was passed.[23] What to

---

[18] MS 979.1. Newell answered this speech with one of his own in which he said, "For ought I know prevented the neck of W. H. Gray testing the strength of a few feet of Uncle Sam's hemp."

[19] Carey, op.cit., I:342.

[20] Oregon Archives, p. 38.

[21] Ibid., pp. 39, 40.

[22] Ibid., pp. 43, 44.

[23] Dr. Elijah White, sub-Indian agent, spoke in favor of the bill, maintaining that under the provisions of the statutes of Iowa the sale of liquor in Indian territory was illegal. Therefore he confiscated a still which he found in the territory. It was necessary to have an agreement on policy

do with "ardent spirits" caused much controversy in later years. Though Newell was one of the later opponents of prohibition in Oregon, there seems to be no record of any opposition to this first attempt to prohibit the introduction of alcohol.

The legislative session lasted for nine days, beginning with June 18, 1844, and then adjourning until December 16, 1844. But when the legislature reconvened on that day, only four members were present. Without a quorum, the meeting was adjourned. On the following day the executive committee presented a report detailing the progress of the negotiations between Great Britain and the United States relative to the Oregon boundary. The opening paragraph of the message summed up the situation:

> As the expectation of receiving some information from the United States, relative to the adjustment of the claims of that government, and of Great Britain, upon this country, was the principal cause of the adjournment of this assembly, from June last to this day, we feel it our duty to communicate such information as we have been able to collect on the subject, and likewise to recommend the adoption of further measures for the promotion and security of the interests of Oregon.[24]

The committee recommended the framing and adoption of a constitution "which may serve as a more thorough guide to her officers and a more firm basis of her laws;" the erection of a public jail; provisions for filling public offices when vacated; provision for settling land claims reserved by Indians; and some boundary changes which would "not conflict with the act passed in this assembly, in June 1843 extending the limits of Oregon to 54° 50' north latitude."[25]

The legislative committee responded to the need for more adequate government and more funds by amending the organic act.

---

in the matter – which the legislature temporarily achieved. See Carey, op.cit., I:342. For a discussion of the adoption of Iowa laws by Oregon see F. L. Herriot, "Transplanting Iowa's Laws to Oregon," O.H.Q. (June, 1904), V:140-150.

[24] Oregon Archives, p. 57.

[25] Ibid..

Provision was made for a light tax – voluntary contributions had turned out to be a theoretical ideal. Those who agreed with the laws passed by the governing body could support the government by their gifts, but if they disagreed they could withhold support. The trouble with this system proved to be lack of sufficient gifts. The precocious government feared a large taxation might alienate enough supporters to make enforcement impossible, so the tax had to be small and the wording of the law as innocuous as possible. A poll tax of fifty cents for all male descendents of a white man, with a tax of one-eighth of one percent on certain property was the final decision. To put teeth in the law, it was provided that those who refused to pay were to be deprived of the protection of the government and were not to be allowed to vote.[26] The task of collecting the first taxes fell to Joe Meek as sheriff, and since he had considerable difficulty, he was granted an additional five months to finish his collecting.

The first tax report gives some interesting information regarding the possessions of the early inhabitants. Dr. John McLoughlin paid the greatest amount of the four hundred on the tax roll, $15.77 on property valued at $12, 212. Robert Newell paid $2.31 on the following property: town lots valued at $800, clocks $12, watches $100, horses $200, mules $300, cattle $20, hogs $20, with a total valuation of $1,452. Only twenty-five of the four hundred taxpayers owned property valued higher than Newell's. After three short years in Oregon, Newell was among the most wealthy, judging from the property he owned.[27]

The executive committee also recommended that the executive power be invested in a single executive rather than in a "triumvirate." It was felt necessary to increase the representation of the people in the government by increasing the number of legislators. The new body was to be called a house of representatives.[28] With these and other changes in the organic law the legislators submitted to the people the question of a constitutional convention. When the returns were counted, it

---

[26] P. and T. papers No. 12191; Oregon Archives, p. 46; Bancroft, op. cit., p. 443.

[27] Oregon Tax Roll, 1844; Original Journal of the Provisional Government 1844; MS 12203, p. 126.

[28] "The Organic Laws of Oregon with Amendments," P. and T. Papers No. 1096.

appeared that the convention was voted down, but that the amended organic law was accepted.[29]

The amended organic law was accepted on July 25, 1845, and the new House of Representatives met for the first time on August 5, 1845, with Newell as a member. The executive power was entrusted to Governor George Abernethy, a steward of the Methodist mission. With a total of 228 votes, Abernethy had defeated Osborne Russell by 98 votes, W. J. Bailey by 153 votes, and A. L. Lovejoy by 157 votes.[30] The governor's salary was set at $300 per year, and each member of the house received $2 per day for every day's attendance, and "ten cents per mile for every mile they necessarily travel in going to and returning from the place of meeting."[31]

To meet the problem of dual sovereignty under which it still labored, the legislature of 1845 fashioned its oath as follows: "I do solemnly swear that I will support the Organic Laws of the Provisional Government of Oregon, so far as the said Organic Laws are consistent with my duties as a citizen of the United States, or a subject of Great Britain and faithfully demean myself in office so help me God."[32]

Government by the amended Organic Law proved to be "strong without an army or navy, rich without a treasury . . . property was safe, schools established and supported, contracts enforced, debts collected and the majesty of the law vindicated."[33]

The year 1845 was a year of important events in Newell's life. In addition to his duties in a legislature with added members and more legislation to consider, he was involved in other interests. His family had increased to six with the birth of Thomas Jefferson Newell on November 25, 1843.[34] With the other settlers in Oregon, Newell had felt the need for a means of circulating local news, reports from the States, and the proceedings of the legislature. The first expression of the feeling was the Oregon Lyceum of 1843. By 1844 the members of the Lyceum decided that "There being no

---

[29] Carey, op.cit., I:346.

[30] Ibid..

[31] "An act fixing the salary of the governor and the per diem pay of members of the House of Representatives," P. and T. Papers No. 1185.

[32] Oregon Archives, p. 71.

[33] Quoted by Robertson, op.cit., p. 39.

[34] Newell Diary, 1829.

printing press or public news paper in this territory – We the undersigned in order to promote science, temperance, morality and general intelligence agree to secure a press and commence the publication of a monthly semi-monthly or weekly papers."[35] The minutes of this meeting went on to define the use of the press. "The press owned by or in connection with this association now called the Oregon Printing Association shall never be used by any party for the purpose of propagating sectarian principles or doctrines nor for the discussion of exclusive party politics."[36]

A drawing of Robert Newell, 1857, Oregon Lyceum
Courtesy of Salem Public Library, Salem, Oregon

The difficulties of printing a newspaper in Oregon at this early date were considerable. Since the population was small, the necessity of providing a regular income to defray the expense of the salary of an editor was a problem. Transportation from the East added a good deal to the amount of money necessary to buy a press. Subscriptions to the press fund totaled eight hundred dollars, with David Leslie and Robert Newell contributing the larges sums – fifty

---

[35] Original Minutes of the Oregon Lyceum Club, Oregon Historical Society MS No. 655 (Hereafter cited as Lyceum Minutes). Turnbull states that the "Printing Association" was formed in 1845, but the original minutes clearly show October 2, 1844, as the date of its beginning under the name.
[36] Ibid. T. C. Elliott, op.cit., p. 109, observes that this statement sounds very much like Newell.

dollars each. "Mr. Newell was requested to assist in procuring stockholders until one thousand dollars be subscribed.[37]Meek was chosen collector for the association, with the agreement that he should received "two and one half percent for his trouble."[38] Governor George Abernethy was elected treasurer and entrusted with the money raised by the association. Abernethy sent the money east where a hand press was secured, with type and the other necessities essential to printing.

Newell's labors for the press and the legislature were interrupted by the death of his Nez Perce wife. Though he recorded only the year of her death,[39] it must have occurred some time in December 1845, for on December 11 he asked to be excused from his duties as Speaker of the House[40] because his wife was "very ill." Some time then between December 11 and January 1, 1846, she must have passed away, ending the union, which had begun in 1833.

Just how Newell felt about his marriage to an Indian while he was married he does not say.[41] The paucity of references to her

---

[37] Lyceum Minutes.

[38] Ibid., No. 655-10. 0-14.

[39] Newell Diary, 1829.

[40] He had been elected speaker of the house on December 2, 1845, and served until December 11, when his wife's illness forced him to leave. The Legislature convened through December 19, but Newell did not participate after the 11th.

[41] Twenty years after his Indian wife had died, Newell in one short sentence left the only indication, which clarifies somewhat the question of how he felt about his marriage to an Indian. In 1865 his son Marcus Whitman had for some misdemeanor been placed in jail in Idaho. Newell wrote to the governor of Idaho Territory to explain why the boy had been placed in jail and to ask for his release. The boy was guilty, he admitted, but guilty because a Mr. Davidson had gotten him "pretty drunk" and "induced him to steel . . . Marcus is young and has a fine chance up here Lewiston, Idaho Territory among his people the Nez Perce Indians. The principal or head chief is a relative of Marcus and gave me his niece for a wife which I probably unfortunately took, in good faith and have done my duty, and still wish to do what is my duty to those dependent on me." Newell to Governor Gibbs, July 7, 1865, Oregon Historical Society.

This statement seems to indicate that in 1865 Newell regretted having married an Indian. However, he may have been influenced by the social status or the misbehavior of his half-breed children. It was written twenty years after the death of his first wife and he had remarried, so it is may have been typical of Newell, for he does not mention his other wives, who were white, in any more than a cursory remark here and there. There is nothing to indicate that he was not a faithful and devoted husband to his native wife and a considerate father to their children.

It is possible that his wife was not well during the last few years of her life, and for this or other reasons, two of the young boys were placed in the home of Alvin T. Smith in July of 1843. The agreement signed by Newell and Smith shows the concern of a father for his children: "To all concerned be it known by these presents that for consideration here after specified I, Alvin T. Smith have received into my family the two little sons of Robert Newell, William M. now five years of age . . . and Marcus W. now three years of age." Smith and his wife agreed to "take a parental interest by means of family instruction, appropriate control in the physical, moral and intellectual improvements of the above named . . ."[42] The charge was one hundred and four dollars per year. Provision was made for renewal of the agreement after one year.[43]

The year 1846 saw another increase in Newell's duties in the government and the community around Oregon City. He was elected one of three directors of the Oregon Printing Association. "After the organization of said board of directors it was deemed expedient to employ an editor. For the purpose of ascertaining who and upon what terms a committee of three was appointed consisting of Robert Newell, J. E. Long and J. W. Nesmith . . ."[44] Newell was

---

not a valid indication of his feeling about the matter during his first marriage.

Newell evidently did not countenance divorce, for in several instances he voted against granting one to those who had petitioned the legislature for one. See Oregon Archives, p. 101. In 1846 Newell was appointed on a special committee to consider a divorce request from Elizabeth Gilliham. The report of the committee was made by Newell, who asked to be discharged from further duty regarding the matter. See Ibid., p. 170.

[42] MS No. 186. The original agreement between Newell and Smith, in Oregon Historical Society. The smiths were Congregationalist, but came to Oregon as independent missionaries and settled in the valley in 1841.

[43] There is no indication when the children were returned to Newell. The census report of 1850 indicates that they were living with him in that year.

[44] Spectator, April 2, 1846. The constitution of the Oregon Printing Association was further elaborated in 1845. Newell was elected in the

chairman of the committee, but due to absence could not serve. Acting in Newell's place, J. E. Long secured the services of William G. T'Vault, president of the association, as editor. T'Vault was to be paid beginning January 1, 1846, at the rate of three hundred dollars per year.[45]

At last, on the fifth day of February 1846, the first newspaper issued in American territory west of the Rocky Mountains was printed. Robert Newell had been influential in making the publication possible, at first by his membership in the Falls Association, later by his interest in the Oregon Lyceum, and finally by his contribution to the Oregon Printing Association and his advice as one of the three on the board of directors. The paper had a somewhat fitful existence until the final issue in 1855; seven different editors and nine printers served on it through the nine years of its publication.

By 1846 Newell had acquired quite a list of "firsts" in the Oregon Country. He had been the first to bring wagons to the Willamette Valley. He was an active participant in the first government organized west of the Rockies. He was a member of the first legislative committee and the first House of Representatives. He belonged to the first literary and debating club, the Oregon Lyceum, and he was influential in publishing the first newspaper west of the Rockies. In addition, he placed the first keel boats in the Willamette river above the falls at Oregon City in 1846.[46] Two years previously Newell had decided to locate on a navigable stream and bought a 640-acre farm near Champoeg from Walter Pomeroy. Though the farm was later registered as a donation land claim, at the time he acquired the land there was no land office to record the sale.[47] This was Newell's home until he moved to Idaho in 1867.[48]

---

following year to the first board of directors called for by the new constitution. See Lyceum Minutes, No. 655, 0-15. George H. Himes, "Historical Tablet at Oregon City," O.H.Q. (September, 1919), XX:297.

[45] T"Vault to the board of directors of the Oregon Printing Association, No. 655, 1-25, Oregon Historical Society.

[46] Randall V. Mills, Stern-Wheelers up the Columbia (Palo Alto, California: Pacific Books, 1944), p. 12.

[47] See Donation land claim No. 2051. The legal description of the farm is Sec. 1-2 and 11 township. 4 S. Range 2 W.

[48] Oregonian, March 6, 1867.

The necessity of providing adequate transportation for the wheat produced in the plains around Champoeg led Newell to fit out the keel boats Mogul and Ben Franklin. To make known his new enterprise, Newell put a typical advertisement in the Spectator for the "Passengers Own Line:"

> The subscriber begs leave to inform the public that he has well caulk'd gumm'd and greas'd the light draft and fast running boats, Mogul and Ben Franklin, now in port for freight or charter, which will ply regularly between Oregon City and Champoeg during the present season.
>
> Passage gratis by paying 50 cents specie or $1. on the stores. Former rules will be observed, passengers can board with the captain by finding their own provisions.
>
> N. B. punctuality to the hour of departure is earnestly requested. As time waits for no man the boats will do the same.[49]

The keel boats were equipped with sails and prepared to meet stubborn winds or calms by having a crew of Indians that could "pull sweeps."

The advent of these ships caused quite a furor in the little community where such a mode of transportation was considered modern indeed. The Spectator warmly approved the advance in transportation facilities:

> In the march of improvements in our infant colony that of boat conveyance is fast progressing. We beg to call the attention of the public to two well built and commodius boats and of superior mould now employed between Oregon City and Champoeg. They ply twice a week upon our beautiful stream exporting "the staff of life" from our fertile plains above and importing returns from below . . . We have paid a visit to the "Mogul" and "Franklin" and

---

[49] Spectator, April 30, 1846.

can testify to the ample and roomy space allotted abaft, for the comfort of from 15 to 20 passengers and from what we have heard expressed by those who have made the passage, and our own personal knowledge of the captain of the "Great Mogul" much is added to the pleasure of the trip through his kindness, polite attention and urbanity. The passage averages during all weather from seven to ten hours. The sailing and pulling qualities of the craft are also first rate . . . . The fare (50 cents) we consider very moderate considering there is no opposition. We conclude by assuring our readers that the passage is rendered perfectly safe, through the nautical knowledge of Captain Flooke of the "Franklin" who is an experienced pilot through all the shoals, rocks and snags of the river . . . .[50]

The transportation around the falls at Oregon City was accomplished by oxen and wagons. Medorum Crawford entered into some sort of an agreement with Newell and a Captain Cook, who operated the "Callipooia" between Oregon City and Vancouver.[51] This combination enabled its owners to monopolize the carrying trade of the country and the portage at the falls.

During the first harvest season in which the boats operated, the Mogul and the Franklin moved 15,000 bushels of wheat from Champoeg, a considerable amount of wheat for the time.[52] James W. Nesmith said that this monopoly was so complete that "nothing like it was ever known in this country until later and wealthier companies, aided by the power of steamers, held all the passes upon both rivers."[53] The success of the enterprise is evident from the advertisement printed in the Spectator on December 10, when the boats had been operating less than a year: "Passengers Own Line – Mogul and B. Franklin. – We beg leave to tender our thanks to the public for the liberal support received during the last season."[54]

---

[50] Mills, op.cit., p. 12.
[51] O.P.A.T. 1880, p. 15.
[52] Spectator, November 12, 1846.
[53] J. W. Nesmith Annual address, O.P.A.T. 1880, p. 15.
[54] Spectator, December 10, 1846.

The monopoly was good while it lasted, but with the coming of steamboats the keel boats were outmoded and inefficient. The first steam boat on the upper Willamette was the Hoosier, built at Salem in 1851.[55] The Lot Whitcomb was built at Milwaukie in 1850 and launched on Christmas Day. The great day was celebrated with instrumental and vocal music, dancing, and feasting in the town of Milwaukie, which welcomed strangers from far and near to the gala event.[56]

Sidewheeler "Lot Whitcomb", built in Milwaukie, Oregon in 1850
Courtesy of Salem Public Library, Salem, OR

Captain Newell, as he was called for a time while active in the shipping business, left a vivid description of the new steamboat, obviously a wonder to those accustomed to the slow-moving keel boats:

She was a splendid sight, certainly a perfect streak, and when under way, I could compare her to nothing but a snow slip rushing down the mountain,

[55] "Early Navigation on the Willamette," Oregonian, November 11, and 18, 1900. The first steamboat in Oregon was the Columbia, built at Astoria in 1850. O.P.A.T. 1878, p. 20. Corning, Willamette Landings Ghost Towns of the River (Portland: Binford and Mort, 1947), p. 25, states that Newell's boats were flatboats and that he owned three, adding the Great Western in May, 1846.
[56] O.P.A.T. 1878, p. 21.

taking all before it; her wheels invisible, the bank of
foam at her bow, her fore and aft flag at full length
stretched out as though nailed to a wall . . . she was
to all appearance splitting the river quite in two and
her waves rolling to the other shore . . . when she
struck up the current, I thought never had suds been
made on so grand a scale. . .[57]

As beautiful as was this sight it signaled the end of the profitable
business enterprise, which Newell had begun in 1846. It had proved
a financial success and increased his already substantial wealth.

On the 28th of June, 1846, Newell married Rebecca
Newman, and event noted in the Spectator of July 4: "Married on
Sunday Evening 28th ult imo by J. M. Garrison, Esq. Capt. Robert
Newell to Miss Rebbecca, eldest daughter of Samuel Newman all of
Champoeg County." The second Mrs. Newell became the mother
of eleven children to increase Newell's family to fifteen children.[58]

There was considerable political activity in 1846. The
people of Oregon hoped that American jurisdiction would be
extended to them immediately after Polk had been successfully
elected on the slogan, "54-40 or fight." But it was two long years
before a treaty was signed between Great Britain and the United
States and a boundary for the area located.

The British sloop-of-war Modeste was sent to Vancouver in
the fall of 1845 to ascertain the condition of the post at Vancouver
and to find out the sentiment of the people in regard to British
sovereignty. The ship remained until the early months of 1846.
Lieut. William Peel, a son of Sir Robert Peel, and another of the
ship's officers attended a house-warming at the new grist mill built
by Dr. McLoughlin at Oregon City:[59]

---

[57] Spectator, July 29, 1851.
[58] Family record of Robert Newell, Appendix I, copied from the vertical
file, Oregon Historical Society. Miss Newman was a student at Mrs.
Thornton's boarding school in Oregon City during her courtship with
Newell. The census report of 1850 lists her age as 18. MS 310, Oregon
Historical Society. See Alice Henson Ernst, "Stage Annals of Early
Oregon From 1846 to 1875," O.H.Q. (June, 1941), XLII:151-161.
[59] McLoughlin resigned his position as Chief Factor in 1846. See "Copy of
a Document," O.P.A.T. 1888, pp. 46-56.

There was a brilliant assemblage of the "fair sex" of Oregon and although in the far west yet from the gay display that night, we are proud to state that the infant colony can boast of as pretty faces and handsome figures as the mother country . . . Reels, country dances, figures eight, and jigs was the order of the evening; and if we do not yet claim that fashionable dance the polka. Still we live in hopes of seeing it soon introduced at our city balls . . . [60]

While at this ball Lieutenant Peel and some of the officers accompanying him became "a little too free in their actions with some of the half breed girls" present.

Doctor Newell called the Lieutenant aside and gave him a word of warning. The Lieutenant replied, "I really did no harm, Doctor," and Newell answered, "No Lieutenant, but you know you would not have acted in that manner with a young lady of your own class in London." "Well Doctor," said Peel, "let us try some other kind of amusement. I will bet you a bottle of wine that more of the men on this floor will in the case of a contest support the British than the American." Doctor Newell accepted the wager without hesitation and when the vote was counted the Americans prevailed. Peel was not to be outdone so easily, and bet Newell "another bottle of wine that the man who has just come in and is standing across the floor there will fight on our side anyhow." The man appeared English but was actually a friend of Newell's, and again the Lieutenant lost, for when asked under which country he would fight, he replied, "I fight under the stars and stripes." That man was Willard H. Rees.[61]

The boundary question was finally settled by the proclamation of the treaty on August 5, 1846, and the 49th parallel was agreed upon as the boundary west of the Rocky Mountains.[62]

---

[60] Spectator, February 19, 1846.

[61] O.P.A.T. 1874, pp. 26-27. T. C. Elliott, op.cit., p. 112.

[62] Treaties and Conventions, pp. 438-439. For a complete discussion of the boundary controversy see Lyman, op.cit., Vol. III. The treaty was signed June 15, 1846, and proclaimed August 5, 1846. See also Brown, op.cit., pp. 229-294.

When the legislature met on December 2, 1846, Governor Abernethy informed them that "the senate ratified the treaty upon the Oregon question by a vote of 41-14."[63] He further explained that formal notice had been given Great Britain in 1845 that the joint occupancy treaty was abrogated by the United States, and that in a matter of a few months the jurisdiction of the United States would be extended to the Oregon Country. Under such conditions he left the legislature to decide upon adjournment after only the most pressing business was transacted.[64] He recommended the consideration of the liquor law, which had proved defective. The organic law stated that the legislature had power to "regulate the introduction, manufacture or sale of ardent spirits."[65] Some held that this did not grant power to prohibit the introduction, manufacture or sale of ardent spirits. Newell was placed on a select committee to consider the act.[66] There was an attempt by Mr. Tolmie to declare the manufacture and sale of ardent spirits illegal, but this was voted down, with Newell one of the "nays."[67] The legislature finally decided that a licensing law was the answer and framed a bill only to have Abernethy veto it and advise a public vote on the issue. The legislature proceeded to pass the measure over the governor's veto.[68]

The location of the capital was an important issue in the legislature of 1846, though the problem assumed greater proportions in the 1850's. Governor Abernethy advertised in the Spectator of November 26, 1846:

> Pursuant to a law passed at the last session of the legislature I hereby give notice that sealed

---

[63] Oregon Archives, p. 158. Carey, op.cit., p. 356, points out that Abernethy did not know of the final treaty; however, he was in possession of a newspaper which stated that the treaty was "probably concluded" and the provisions of the treaty in regard to the boundary were explained at the meeting of the legislature December 2, 1846.

[64] Ibid., p. 159.

[65] Ibid., p. 159-160.

[66] Ibid., p. 184.

[67] Ibid., p. 186.

[68] Spectator, December 24, 1846, full text of the veto message and voting record. Also Oregon Archives, pp. 198, 199. Governor Abernethy suggested that only enough alcohol be allowed in the country for medicinal purposes.

proposals endorsed, "proposals for locating the seat of Government" will be received at the secretaries office until Monday the 30th day of November next from all persons who may desire to give donations to the Government for the purpose of erecting Public Buildings and locating the seat of Government.

One of those offered land for the erection of the public buildings needed by the governing body was Robert Newell. His offer was "one block in Champoeg," which he stated was "thought to be the most central place for a seat of government.[69] He also offered thirty lots "exclusive of the public square to be taken promiscuously within the plot but none of the 30 lots shall be the worst of the lots in the place."[70]

With the coming of 1847 political activity was unusually intense. The terms of the treaty with Great Britain were known for certain, but it was not known whether or not the United States would send a new set of officers who were non-residents to govern the territory.

Governor Abernethy, the representative of the mission interests,[71] was opposed in the election of 1847 by A. L. Lovejoy, the independent candidate. Sixteen votes reelected Abernethy in a count of 520. Newell was again elected representative from Champoeg County, and chosen speaker of the house on December 8, 1847; of the seventeen votes Newell received fourteen. In a brief and appropriate manner, he returned his thanks to the house.[72] He reached his peak as a legislator and a politician in this office. Among his duties was the appointment of various committees, the

---

[69] Original proposal in Newell's handwriting, MS 677, Oregon Historical Society. It is rather ironical that the site considered the logical choice for the capital by Newell was completely inundated in 1861 and today is marked only by historical interest.

[70] Ibid.,

[71] Governor Abernethy was nominally the head of the American party when there was an opposition from the Hudson's Bay influence. By 1847 the Hudson's Bay people had fused with the Americans awaiting jurisdiction of the United States. See Bradley, op.cit., p. 63.

[72] Oregon Archives, p. 221. The Spectator, December 9, 1847, took note of the election and remarked that "The House of Representatives has been organized by the election of Robert Newell of Champoeg as speaker.

signing of all bills that became law, and an effort to harmonize the divergent tendencies of the house of representatives. Since his first experience in the legislative committee of 1843 (when he had confessed he was quite ignorant of the process of law-making), he had learned a good deal. If he still lacked the knowledge of many of the technicalities needed to be a great parliamentarian, he did have a natural ability "to hold in check extreme measures and to harmonize differences by his prudence and sense of fairness and jovial good will."[73]

An amusing example of Newell's ignorance of parliamentary tactics is related by J. W. Nesmith, a member of the 1847 legislature. Mr. Nesmith was quite sure that he would be elected speaker of this legislature, but he said, "Some of my friends threw off on me and elected a better man, in the person of Dr. Robert Newell. God Bless his old soul." Nesmith found a copy of Jefferson's manual in the library at the Falls known as Multnomah Library and studied the work carefully on the usage of "the previous question." He had presented a bill to cut off the southern end of Yamhill and to establish the county of Polk, but the measure had met violent opposition in the House. This legislative session was held in the Methodist Church at the Falls, and close by the church a man by the name of Barton Lee had constructed a "ten pin alley" where some of the legislature "were in the habit of resorting to seek relaxation and refreshment from their legislative toils." One morning while most of his opponents were amusing themselves at horse billiards in the tenpin alley, Nesmith called up his bill and gave a speech in its support after which he said:

> And now Mr. Speaker upon this bill I move the previous question. Newell looked confused and I was satisfied that he had no conception of what I meant; but he rallied and looking wise and severe (I have since seen presiding officers in Washington do the same thing) said "Sit down Sir. Resume your seat! Do you intend to trifle with the chair when you knew we passed the previous question two weeks ago? It was the first thing we done." I got a vote however before the return of the "horse billiard" players, and polk county has a legal

---

[73] Quoted by Dobbs, <u>Men of Champoeg</u>, p. 152.

existence today, notwithstanding the adverse ruling upon a question of parliamentary usage."[74]

That Newell's parliamentary blunders did not affect his prominent place in the community is evidenced by the various positions he held in 1847 outside of the government. He was elected chairman of a group of farmers from Champoeg County who met "for the purpose of discussing the propriety of creating an exporting company. The opinion of the number assembled was that all in their vicinity would join in the work."[75]

The land question caused much concern, for those settlers who had taken claims by the section lines established under the Organic act were fearful lest the new boundary settlement establish sections at variance with the original lines. Settlers were arriving in large numbers each year and a definite principle was needed to establish land claims. In consequence, "a very numerous and respectable body of citizens assembled at the city hotel at half past seven o'clock p.m." Doctor Newell addressed the group and was one of a committee of five appointed "to select twelve whose duty it shall be to investigate and adjudicate between disputing claimants."[76]

On November 29, 1847, Doctor and Mrs. Whitman and eight others at the Waiilatpu mission were killed by the Indians,[77] an event which excited and alarmed the community in the Willamette Valley. The remaining inhabitants of the mission were held captive for approximately a month. The brutalities suffered by the men and the indignities forced upon the women while captives of the savages form an unpleasant chapter in the history of the Pacific Northwest.

---

[74] J. W. Nesmith, O.P.A.T. 1875, pp. 59-60.
[75] Spectator, March 18, 1847.
[76] Ibid., May 27, 1847.

[77] There were nine deaths besides the Whitmans as a result of the massacre on the 29th. Helen Mar Meek, the daughter of Joe Meek, had been left at the mission in 1840; she was ill at the time of her capture and died of neglect. For a full account of the massacre, see Drury, Marcus Whitman, Pioneer and Martyr; Victor, River of the West, and Early Indian Wars of Oregon (Salem: Franck C. Baker State Printer, 1894), pp. 92-126 (Hereafter cited Indian Wars). Brown, op.cit., p. 315, gives the date of the massacre as Oct. 27, 1847. This date is not corroborated by the other accounts.

Newell had warned Dr. Whitman to leave the mission because the Indians disliked him. Rev. J. B. A. Brouillet, Catholic vicar-general of Walla Walla, prepared a memorial to Congress, in which he stated that,

> Mr. Newell now speaker of the legislature of the territory, who lived with the Nez Perces and who had an opportunity of knowing the Cayuses well, often said to Dr. Whitman during these last years that he ought to leave Wailatpu, because the Indians hated him and would kill him. He told me himself speaking of Dr. Whitman and Mr. Spalding that he was astonished that they had stood so long. Mr. Spalding would have been killed long ago said he if it had not been for his wife, who was very much liked by the Indians.[78]

More important perhaps than the Indians' feeling toward the individual missionaries was their growing resentment at the ever-increasing number of settlers from the East. Not only did the whites take Indian land, they brought with them diseases to which the Indians were very susceptible.

News of the massacre was communicated to the House of Representatives convening at Oregon City on Wednesday, December 8, 1847.[79] This unexpected event called for immediate action and the House responded by passing the following act: "Resolved that governor is herby required to raise arms and equip a company of riflemen, not to exceed fifty men with their captain and subaltern officers, and dispatch them forthwith to occupy the mission station at the Dalles, on the Columbia river, and hold possession of the same until reinforcements can arrive at that point, or other means to be taken as the government may think advisable."[80] Two days later the legislature approved a resolution to send a special messenger to Washington to secure "the immediate

---

[78] House Executive Documents No. 38, 35th Congress, 1st session, Series 955, pp. 2-26. At the time Brouillet wrote there was an attempt to fasten the blame for the massacre on the Catholics by certain of the Protestant missionaries, in particular, H. H. Spalding.

[79] Oregon Archieves, p. 223.

[80] Ibid.

influence and protection of the United States government in our internal affairs in view of the critical situation existing with the Indians."[81]

In order to carry out such a program it was necessary to have money, a commodity scarce in Oregon at this date. To meet this need a commission consisting of Jesse Applegate, A. L. Lovejoy and George L. Curry were empowered to negotiate a loan "not to exceed one hundred thousand dollars." The Hudson's Bay Company was the only organization with sufficient resources to advance a loan of that size, but they answered the request of the loan commission by claiming lack of authority to grant such a loan.[82] Governor Abernethy, Jesse Applegate, and A. L. Lovejoy borrowed on their own credit nearly one thousand dollars in supplies with which to furnish the volunteer company of riflemen, which had been ordered to The Dalles. Governor Abernethy asked aid from the merchants of Oregon City suggesting that the United States Government would without doubt assume the debt later.[83]

Despite the Company's refusal to advance a loan, Peter Skene Ogden, an official at Vancouver, left the fort on December 7 with a party of sixteen men to attempt to rescue the survivors. After some debating with the Cayuse chiefs, Ogden was successful in ransoming the captives.

The Company's position was a difficult one, for they were dependent upon the good will of the Indians for their business success. If they should put an armed force into the field against the Indians or actively support an American offensive, their chance of successful fur-gathering was small. The Indians could not hunt and trap while engaged in a war. Yet at least for the sake of example and discipline among the Indians the deed deserved punishment; to refuse aid in accomplishing this punishment would incur the wrath of the American settlers. Probably the course of action followed by

---

[81] Ibid., p. 225.

[82] There had been trouble between Dr. McLoughlin and the Hudson's Bay Company over McLoughlin's generous aid to the American settlers, which, with other differences, resulted in McLoughlin's resignation in 1845. See Frederick V. Holman, Dr. John McLoughlin, The Father of Oregon (Cleveland: A. H. Clark Co., 1907), p. 90. Victor suggests that a loan to the Americans appeared to mean war with the Indians, which would injure the trade of the Company and possibly mean a reprimand from the Company officials. See Indian Wars, p. 135.

[83] Spectator, December 10, 1847.

the company was the best possible. In addition to Ogden's rescue, James Douglas, chief factor at Vancouver, loaned supplies to the government through individuals.[84]

The Provisional Government was faced with the task of punishing the savages, and at the same time of preventing a coalition of all the Indians in the area, a possibility which had frightening potentialities. The volunteer company of fifty men under H. A. G. Lee stationed at The Dalles was insufficient to successfully prosecute a war against several tribes. More troops had to be mustered and more money acquired for equipment. The little community of settlers found themselves faced with an Indian war. The urgent memorial passed by the legislature on December 10, 1847, asking aid from Washington indicates the gravity of the situation.

> Having called upon the government of the United States so often in vain we have almost despaired of receiving its protection, yet we trust that our present situation, when fully laid before you will at once satisfy your honorable body of the great necessity of extending the strong arm of guardianship and protection over this remote, but beautiful portion of the United States domain. Our relations with the proud and powerful tribes of Indians residing east of the Cascade mountains . . . have recently assumed quite a different character. They have shouted the war-whoop and crimsoned their tomahawks in the blood of our citizens . . . .

> Called upon to resent this outrage, we feel sensibly our weakness and inability to enter a war with powerful tribes of Indians . . . . Circumstances warrant your memorialists in believing that many of the powerful tribes inhabiting the upper valley of the Columbia, have formed an alliance for the purpose of carrying on hostilities against our settlements. The number of white population in Oregon is alarmingly insignificant compared with the swarms of Indians, which throng its valleys.

---

[84] Bancroft, op.cit., pp. 672, 675.

To repel the attacks of so formidable a foe, and protect our families and property from violence and raping will require more strength than we possess. We are deficient in many of the grand essentials of war -- such as men, arms and treasure; for then our sole reliance is on the government of the United States; we have the right to expect your aid and you are in justice bound to extend it . . . .[85]

In conclusion Meek was presented to the congress with a request that he be reimbursed for his conveyance of the message.

The legislature did not wait to act until they received word from Washington. On December 14, a resolution was passed which meant an important appointment for Newell, though he did not know at the time that he would be involved. It was resolved "that a delegation of three persons be appointed by this house to proceed immediately to Walla Walla and hold a council with the chiefs and principal men of the various tribes on the Columbia to prevent if possible their coalition with the Cayuse tribe in the present difficulties."[86]

Governor Abernethy had thought a small force sufficient to protect the property at The Dalles, but at the threat of a coalition of the tribes he called on the citizens to furnish five hundred men. This force was thought necessary to prevent further loss of immigrant property. There was also a great deal of fear among the settlers, especially in the more remote sections, who "feared to go to sleep . . and the father of the household kept watch beside his arms not knowing but their safty depended on his sleeplessness. The Indians took advantage of this state of things to exhibit unusual insolence and even to make threats and circulate terrifying rumors."[87] To finance the little army the loan commission called a meeting of the citizens of Oregon City, who pledged one thousand dollars. Another thousand dollars was acquired from George Roberts, superintendent of the Oregon mission, and sixteen hundred dollars was pledged by the merchants of Oregon City.[88]

---

[85] For full text see Brown, op.cit., pp. 335, 336.
[86] Oregon Archives, p. 230.
[87] Indian Wars, p. 153.
[88] "Report of the loan commission," Indian Wars, pp. 139-140.

The missionaries, Spalding, Craig, and Father Blanchet, and Ogden sent word urging that the government refrain from sending troops, but the message was slow in arriving at Oregon City, and the resolution was passed in favor of making an army.[89]

The legislative session of 1847 closed without appointing the three commissioners. The last resolution of the 1847 session read: "Resolved that Robert Newell our present speaker, have the thanks of the members of this house, for the able and impartial manner in which he has discharged the duties of speaker."[90] The 1847 legislature was the last in which Newell served as speaker. Though actively engaged in politics the rest of his life, the session of 1847 was the high point of his career as a legislator and politician. Other minor offices, which he held were: assessor in 1844,[91] reviewer of public roads in 1845,[92] and road commissioner, Oregon City to the Island.[93]

---

[89] Elliott, op.cit., p. 115.
[90] Oregon Archives, p. 254.
[91] P. and T. papers, No. 913..
[92] Ibid., p. 937.
[93] Ibid., p. 1404.

CHAPTER V

A MEMBER OF THE "MUZZLING MAJORITY," AND COMMISSIONER TO THE INDIANS

During the official meeting of the House of Representatives in 1847 an incident occurred which involved Newell in a controversy with George L. Curry, a future governor of Oregon. The roots of the argument went back some time before the situation was made public in the <u>Spectator</u> early in 1848.

When the citizens of Oregon learned in 1846 that it was the intention of the United States to discontinue the joint occupation shared with Great Britain and extend the government of the United States to Oregon, a meeting was called to determine the advisability of drafting petitions to be signed by the people and forwarded to Congress. This was done, but the identity of the courier was not decided.[1]

In October 1847, Governor Abernethy secretly dispatched Jesse Quinn Thornton to Washington.[2] Judge James Nesmith of Polk County took official cognizance of the act by presenting a bill on December 15, 1847, censoring Abernethy's action:

> 1st, Whereas, it is believed that the period is at hand when the government of the United States will be extended over Oregon Territory, and officers appointed to administer and execute laws . . . . 2nd, whereas owing to our remote situation and great distance from the capital of the United States, the president thereof is liable to be imposed upon and deceived by the aspirants to office and their friends residing in Oregon and 3rd, whereas it is generally believed that J. Quinn Thornton has been secretly dispatched to Washington City with recommendations, petitions and memorials secretly gotten up for the purpose of obtaining for himself

---

[1] <u>Spectator</u>, September 17, 1846.
[2] Woodward, <u>op.cit.</u>, p. 24.

and friends the high and important offices which will be at the disposal of the president of the United States . . . .

1st, Resolved that it is the duty of this legislature as the immediate representatives of the people of Oregon to use all honorable means to avert such a calamity as the appointment of J. Quinn Thornton or any individual by whom he may be severally recommended to any office of honor or trust within the limits of Oregon Territory . . . .[3]

The vote on the measure resulted in a tie with Newell among those who opposed adoption.

J. Quinn Thornton, 1810-1888, Oregon pioneer, 1848
Ben Maxwell Collection, Courtesy of Salem Public Library
Salem, Oregon

Subsequently, Newell and the other members of the board of directors of the Oregon Printing Association learned that the

---

[3] Spectator, December 25, 1847.

editor of the Spectator, G. L. Curry, planned to print the resolution with the names of those who voted for and against it.

According to Curry's version, Newell came to visit him, stating that he had been selected by the board of directors to speak with Curry regarding certain policies. Curry demanded that any communication be presented in writing. Newell then wrote his message to Curry:

> Whereas information has been communicated to this board that certain resolutions affecting the character of J. Q. Thornton which were brought before the present Legislature and not passed are about to be published in the present No. of the Spectator; therefore: Resolved that Mr. Curry be respectfully requested not to publish said communications, and the more especially as we deem it improper to publish what the legislature has not done until the paper shall have reported to some considerable extent what really has been done by that honorable body.

> Robert Newell
> Chairman of Committee[4]

Curry labeled "Geo. Abernethy, W. Robberts Jr., R. Robb and Robert Newell (who constitute a bare majority of the board of directors of the Printing Association)," the "Muzzling Majority" for the above action.[5] Because Newell's written communication was not addressed specifically to anyone, but only handed to Curry, the editor refused to give an answer. He stated that "if it was any satisfaction to him [Newell] we would say that the paper which would be published the next day would show whether the request had been complied with."[6] About two hours after Curry's ambiguous remarks he was presented the following communication: "Mr. Curry, Sir: There has been a resolution passed the board to this effect; Resolved, that the services of the present editor, G. L. Curry are no longer required, but that his salary be continued for 30

---

[4] Spectator, January 6, 1848.
[5] Ibid.
[6] Ibid.

days without any editorial labor as compensation from this date. J. R. Robb, Sec, Pro. Tem."

After this notice, Curry edited two more issues, which gave him ample opportunity to present the incident from his own side. He did not hesitate to make fun of his employers, and in the last issue he published as editor he said:

> Appointment Extraordinary – The board of directors have appointed George Abernethy and Robert Newell two of the "muzzling majority" to edit the Spectator until they shall have obtained a suitable person to victimize as editor. Our "tripod" will be exceedingly distinguished by such a concentration of talent – They draw together so remarkably well in the editorial harness and Orthography and Syntax will have such a holiday.[7]

Before Abernethy and Newell were forced to act as editors they obtained the service of Aaron E. Wait, who published the next issue on February 10, 1848. Since the two were in agreement with the majority of the directors, they were in a position to answer Curry's charges. Newell made a formal reply in the first issue edited by Wait. Curry, Newell stated, had falsely informed the public that his dismissal was due to the publication of the "Thornton resolutions." This was not the case. The board had met a few days after the annual meeting of the stockholders, and the decision to fire Curry had then been carried. It was the unanimous opinion of the board that the paper "was on the downward march and that it was very unpopular." The board finally decided to have Lovejoy speak to Curry about the matter and suggest that Curry resign, which the latter refused to do. It was then that Curry had published his attack on the members of the board. "What I have done with regard to Mr. Curry, I have done under a sense of duty, and had he been my brother to have taken any other course would in my opinion have been wrong."[8]

---

[7] Spectator, January 20, 1848.
[8] Ibid.

Right or wrong, Curry was fired. He had presented the Thornton resolution and attacked Abernethy and Newell, but with little damage.[9]

With the explanation offered by Newell on February 10, the controversy ceased. In the meantime Governor Abernethy appointed three commissioners[10] to hold a council with the Indians. Those chosen were Joel Palmer, superintendent of Indian affairs;[11] Major H. A. G. Lee, who was at The Dalles in charge of the first army of volunteers sent to protect the mission station;[12] and Robert Newell, "than whom no more competent men for this duty could have been selected among the Americans."[13]

Colonel Cornelius Gilliam, commander of the army, and his subordinate officers were faced with a tremendous task. It was their duty to keep an organized army in the field without transportation except for slow-moving boats or packhorses and wagons, with only scanty food, and poor clothing. And the war was to be carried on some three hundred miles from the settlement where the few provisions available were located. Under such conditions Gilliam

---

[9] It is evident from this and later developments that Newell and Abernethy were substantially in agreement as to governmental policies, but whether or not they deliberately tried to keep the Thornton resolution hushed will have to be decided individually until further evidence is available. It will be remembered that Newell voted against condemning Thornton and there is a strong possibility that as a friend of Abernethy, he did not think publication of an act to censor Abernethy's appointment was politically sagacious. The author has been unable to locate any correspondence that would clarity the problem.

For a critical account of Thornton's mission see F. F. Victor, "Our Public Land System," O.H.Q. (June, 1900), I:148, footnote. A more favorable account of his services is given by H. W. Scott, "The Provisional Government," O.H.Q. (June, 1901), II:114-117; S. A. Clarke, Pioneer Days of Oregon History, 2 Vols. (Portland, Oregon: J. K. Gill Co., 1905), pp. 695, 722.

[10] The Spectator, January 6, 1848, states that the house forgot to appoint these commissioners. Whether through neglect or design, Governor Abernethy appointed these commissioners.

[11] For a complete discussion of Palmer's activity as Indian Superintendent see Stanley S. Spaid, Joel Palmer and Indian Affairs in Oregon, Ph. D. Thesis, University of Oregon, 1950.

[12] Indian Wars, pp. 133, 134.

[13] Ibid., p. 152.

wrote to his wife that he "had to be Colonel, Major, Adjutant, Captain, Seargent and everything else."[14]

Gilliam was probably the best fitted to perform these duties, for he had been in many offices before his appointment as "Colonel Commandant." Bancroft says, "he was brave, obstinate, impetuous and generous . . . . His accomplishments were varied, he had served in the Black Hawk war and also in the Seminole war in Florida as Captain, he had preached the gospel of Christ, he had been a sheriff of a county, and had served in the Missouri legislature. He was indeed just the robust, impulsive, sympathetic, willful and courageous leader the men of the border would choose."[15] He was to need all the experience he had gained from being warrior, sheriff, legislator, and minister.

Gilliam, who had arrived in Oregon in 1844, took seriously Polk's campaign pledge "fifty-four forty or fight." He had definite ideas regarding the rights of the American immigrants as opposed to those of the English. To furnish some much-needed ammunition for his army of two hundred and twenty men, the Colonel, it was rumored, had declared his intention of "pulling down Fort Vancouver about the ears of its inmates."[16] A letter from James Douglas to Governor Abernethy asking for a "distinct disavowal of any such intention" indicates the seriousness of the situation.[17]

Abernethy replied that Gilliam would probably cross the Columbia at the mouth of the Sandy and had no intention of levying contributions from the Hudson's Bay Company.[18]

Gilliam did cross the Columbia at Fort Vancouver, but instead of carrying out his threat, he and Palmer assumed personal responsibility for supplies worth eight hundred dollars. It is

---

[14] Ibid., Quoted in a footnote p. 156.

[15] Bancroft, op.cit., p. 449.

[16] Indian Wars, p. 161. There was particularly strong religious feeling at this time and the Protestant population accused the Hudson's Bay Company of being pro-catholic. Mr. Douglas, chief factor at this time at Vancouver, Mr. Ogden, second in command, Mr. McKinlay, Mr. Ermatinger and others in the company were Protestant, but the long career of McLoughlin, a Catholic, had established the idea among the settlers that the company was primarily Catholic. Colonel Gilliam was an ardent Protestant.

[17] The letter may be found in Brown, op.cit., pp. 338-339.

[18] Ibid., p. 162.

conceivable that a war with England could have resulted had Gilliam acted imprudently.[19]

By January 14 Colonel Gilliam and his army were ready to leave Fort Vancouver. Their supplies were sent up-river in boats, but the troops marched by land to Fort Gilliam, a supply post erected above The Dalles before the army arrived.[20]

The peace commissioners did not leave until February 3rd. The Spectator took note of their departure with an article entitled "Commissioner to the Indians."

> On the 3rd inst. Hon. Robert Newell and Gen. Joel Palmer with Perrin Whitman and two others left this city for The Dalles where they will join Major Lee and proceed into the interior for the purpose of having a talk with the Nez Perces and preventing that and other neighboring tribes from joining the Cayuses in their hostility against the citizens of the valley. Messrs. Newell and Lee go to the Indians in the capacity of commissioners. Mr. Palmer goes in his capacity of Superintendent of Indian affairs. They carry the Pipe of Peace for the acceptance of all those Indians who are not implicated in the murders at Waiilatpu or in the robberies of the immigrants.
>
> Justice requires that the forces now in the field should take effective measures to prevent further aggressions upon immigrants. Stern justice and duty demand punishment of all implicated in the late soul-sickning murders; but mercy as plainly and loudly commands that the wrongs of the guilty should not be visited upon the innocent.[21]

The specific instructions issued to the commissioners are to be found in a letter from Abernethy to the commissioners.[22]

---

[19] Douglas had warned in his letter to Abernethy that he represented "A Powerful British Association." Ibid.

[20] Spectator, January 20, 1848.

[21] Spectator, February 10, 1848.

[22] Brown, op.cit., p. 350.

Gentlemen—the object of appointing you as commissioners to treat with the Nez Perces and other tribes is to avert a general war with the Indians of the upper country and to prevent a union among the tribes as far as possible. To prevent this every effort should be made on your part as far as is consistent with the honor of American citizens. Ther are some requisitions that must be complied with on the part of the Indians and must be insisted on by you. Viz;

All the murderers, and those that forced the young women must be delivered up for punishment, the property taken delivered up or an equivalent given, and restitution made of the property stolen from the immigrants last year, this you cannot ascertain but it can be so arranged that the persons who had property stolen from them can get it hereafter or an equivalent. I am aware the greatest difficulty will be in obtaining the persons of the murderers, but the Indians must be given to understand in the commencement of negotiations that this must be done, that no compromise can be made.

There may be some among those that are implicated in this affair, around whom come paliating circumstances may be thrown, these you will take into consideration. But the principal actors should be executed in the presence of all the tribes.

You will hold a council with the field officers of the army and decide in council, what steps shall be taken to accomplish the most desired object, the restoration of peace. You will use every exertion to have the lives and property of our fellow citizens that may hereafter be traveling through the Indian country, preserved. The chiefs are able to govern their own people. Make as advantageous a treaty with them as you can, binding them to use their influence to protect American citizens.

On your arrival at The Dalles you must be guided by circumstances as to the time and place of meeting the chiefs, but let runners be sent among them, informing them of your intentions and object.

Thus a peace commission and an army was sent to the Indians at the same time. Such a combination was almost a contradiction, and probably Abernethy realized the possibility of friction arising between the two groups, for he wrote a letter to Gilliam advising him that the commissioners had been appointed and asking for complete unity between the officers and the commissioners. In this same communication he left to Gilliam the decision as to whether or not to advance immediately to Waiilatpu and build a fort.[23] The governor's instructions indicate that the commissioners were to try to arrange a settlement before the army took over. In the orders to Gilliam, Abernethy wrote this significant statement: "Should the tribes combine and refuse to comply with the commissioners, I leave the field in your hands."[24]

Gilliam was restless and determined to punish the Indians. Before the main army could reach The Dalles, Lee had of necessity attacked the Indians. Twenty-three Cayuse Indians gathered up the stock around the mission with the intention of driving it away. Lee with seventeen men went in pursuit. Though three Indians were killed and one wounded, the Indians were well mounted and succeeded in driving away three hundred head of cattle—a serious loss to the food potential.[25] When the news reached him, Gilliam outfitted one hundred and thirty men, "All that could be mounted and equipted and led them to the DesChutes river in hopes of finding the stolen animals." This maneuver resulted in several minor skirmishes in which one Indian was killed and one squaw

---

[23] Letter, Abernethy to Gilliam, February 3, 1848, Spectator, April 6, 1848.
[24] Ibid.
[25] This act occurred immediately after Mr. Ogden with the captives passed The Dalles. It was no doubt a retaliation for the presence of armed men in The Dalles. According to the agreement Ogden made with the Cayuse, peace commissioners were to be sent to talk peace during which time no war measures were to be taken. See Inidan Wars, p. 158.

taken captive. In the evening when the Army was returning to camp a mounted and well-armed force of Indians caught the army in a ravine where they proceeded to roll boulders down on them, forcing them to dismount and find shelter, but inflicting no serious damage.

The next day the troops made a more successful attack, killing several Indians and capturing a large number of horses. This day's exploits resulted in the capture of fourteen hundred dollars worth of stolen goods, which the Indians had hidden in the hills. Of the fighting Palmer said that the "yelling of the troops so far exceeded that of the Indians the latter were demoralized and fled from the field."[26]

Considering the condition of the army and their small amount of ammunition, such a method of attack was appropriate—yells were much cheaper than bullets. Wesley Shannon, the ordnance officer, wrote at this time: "The regiment made a heavey draw today before starting in the ammunition line. I have issued about one thousand rounds today which has taken nearly all the rifle powder and lead, percussion caps also very scarce."[27] Gilliam's army lost three men as a result of this expedition; two were decoyed from camp and shot by the Indians, and the third was accidentally shot by the guard.

The army made its way to Fort Gilliam, called by the volunteers "the cabins," where it awaited further orders.

Regardless of the need for unanimity, which Governor Abernethy had requested, the meeting of the officers and the commissioners on February 11 resulted in no agreement. On the 12th a compromise was effected and the commissioners, with enough men to make up a company of one hundred, were allowed to precede the regular army. In accord with Abernethy's request, runners were dispatched to the Indians to acquaint them with the presence of the army and the mission of the peace commissioners.[28] The commissioners had planned to advance on the morning of the 14th, but before peace negotiations could be consummated the war continued without regard to the guilty or innocent.

[26] Indian Wars, p. 166.
[27] Ibid.
[28] Bancroft, op.cit., p. 707.

Newell kept a diary of his experiences on this mission, which gives an indication of the condition of the army.[29] "An Indian was shot today by one of our people, H. English while hunting horses, this day February 13th, a most shameful thing."[30] It was an undisciplined army composed of volunteer troops brought together in a wild country without proper training, and it had a large element of careless adventure-seekers bent on enjoying a new thrill – fighting Indians. Many firmly subscribed to the theory that the only good Indian was a dead one. On February 13 Newell's diary records: "Several men leaving for the settlements. Captain Ross resigned. Many displeased with our people in consequence of bad discipline."[31]

During these days of inactivity the commissioners talked with as many Indians as they could contact to ascertain if possible the general frame of mind of the Indians. On the 14th of February two Yakimas came to the camp to learn the real intentions of the whites, explaining that the Cayuses had been many times to visit the Yakimas since the massacre and had offered gifts of horses and cattle if they would join them, telling them that the whites were coming to kill all the Indians. The Yakimas said they had not troubled the whites, and that the whites had not troubled them because the immigrants used a road, which did not pass through the Yakima country. They expressed regret that the Cayuses had killed Dr. Whitman. The Indians were warmly received and given an exact account of the intentions of the government in dealing with them. There was a general feeling of alarm among the Indians as a result of the presence of so many armed men and to allay their fears the commissioners promised the Indians that no harm would come to the innocent. Little wonder the commissioners frowned on promiscuous shooting by the volunteers or any advance by the army before peace overtures could be made.[32]

---

[29] The writer has been unable to locate this diary. The Bancroft library has a copy someplace, but are unable to locate it since they have rearranged their material. The State of Oregon formerly owned a copy, but it was destroyed when the capitol burned. This work uses the excerpts from the diary given in Bancroft's History of Oregon and Victor's Indian Wars. (Now in University of Oregon Special Collections – 1951)

[30] Bancroft, op.cit., p. 707; quoted from Newell's Diary.

[31] Indian Wars, p. 169.

[32] Report of the Commissioners, Spectator, April 6, 1848. (Hereafter cited Report of Commissioners.)

Gilliam had received word on the 13th that the tribes east of The Dalles had effected a coalition. This news prompted him to take all but a representative force from Fort Gilliam and proceed immediately for Waiilatpu. The peace commissioners asked permission to precede the army as planned, but were disappointed by Gilliam's statement that the danger was so great he could not sacrifice sufficient troops to allow protection for their advance.[33]

Before the army began its march on February 15 the commissioners accomplished two important transactions. First, they were approached by two Indians of the Deschutes tribe who explained that they were forced by the Cayuses to join them in fighting the whites. The Indians were given gifts and asked to meet with the army on the road, as there was not time to wait for them at the fort. Second, they dispatched a messenger to the Nez Perces and Walla Walla Indians asking them to shun the Cayuses and assuring them that the army meant no harm to their people. This message was thought necessary because Gilliam insisted the army should advance without giving the commissioners an opportunity to negotiate. Such a hasty advance might provoke the Nez Perce and Walla Walla Indians into open war.

The messenger chosen as most likely to succeed on such an errand was an Indian who had accompanied Newell and Palmer from Oregon City, "Old Elijah."[34] He was given a flag and a generous amount of tobacco as gifts for the Nez Perces. The old Indian "unfortunately or designedly," in the words of the official report, fell in with the Cayuses who appropriated the flag and tobacco for their own use and destroyed the message to the Nez Perces.

Fortunately, however, two Nez Perces arrived in camp and were given the message, which they hurriedly took to their people. "To this fortunate occurrence we owe perhaps much of our success in preventing a union of these tribes."[35]

Nothing unusual happened during the army's journey from Fort Gilliam to Waiilatpu until the 18th, when it became apparent that a party of the enemy had recently camped in the area. Major Lee was ordered to pursue the savages but returned without sighting

---

[33] Ibid.
[34] Ibid.
[35] Report of Commissioners. The two were Timothy and Red Wolf.

84

them. Discipline continued poor. One entire company considered the possibility of turning back without orders.[36]

On the 23rd a Deschutes arrived with twelve of his men and offered to bring all the stolen property taken from the immigrants if that would make them friends of the whites. Colonel Gilliam finally accepted these terms, though Newell in his diary states that "Gilliam was reluctant to condone the previous conduct of these Indians and would have preferred to fight them."[37]

The troops resented these peace measures too, and it was with difficulty that the Indians were allowed to depart unmolested. Almost two hundred miles from home, the army was poorly fed, poorly equipped and in no mood to continue the strenuous march if its only mission was to accompany peace commissioners. Newell reports regarding the discipline: "Most shocking was this to witness. Some few had bought a little tea and sugar in the settlement to use on the road and many were displeased that they did not share these luxuries with the rest, and objected to their being carried on the public wagons, but the officers set their faces against all such unreasonable objections."[38]

Two Indian spies were spotted on the 24th. The peace commission advanced to meet them displaying a white flag, but the Indians avoided them. Soon a large war party was sighted, indicating unmistakably their intent to fight. The first hostile act was the shooting of a dog belonging to one of the volunteers, which signaled the beginning of the battle. The fight began about noon and lasted until dark, the Indians losing eight killed and five wounded, while Gilliam had five wounded, one seriously.[39]

The Cayuse had boasted they would beat the Americans to death and proceed to the Willamette valley to take their women and property. But their ill success on this first day no doubt dampened their spirits. At the close of the day's fighting Newell remarked that it was easy to distinguish between those who were guilty and those who had no personal interest in the fight and would have avoided it

---

[36] Bancroft, op.cit., p. 708.
[37] Indian Wars, p. 173.
[38] Ibid., p. 173.
[39] This battle took place approximately twenty miles east of Willow Creek. Ibid., pp. 171-173.

if possible. With the Cayuses divided among themselves the remainder of the fighting was cautious and ineffectual.[40]

The army was cut off from water for two days, but considering their difficult position they behaved well. During the second day of fighting some of the Cayuse came close enough to indicate a desire for a peace council, but the army officials and the commissioners agreed such a council could not be held until the army reached water. About sunset of the second day the army arrived at the Umatilla River where the commissioners told Sticcas, Chief of the Cayuse, to meet them at Waiilatpu for a peace council.

From the Umatilla the army moved on the 27th and 28th of February to a place near Fort Walla Walla where Gilliam, Palmer, Newell, and McBean (the latter had knowledge of the dispatches from Vancouver and was supposed to express the sentiments of headquarters) discussed the best method of procedure. According to Newell's diary, McBean was of the opinion that a war could be averted.[41]

On March 2 the army camped near the site of Whitman's mission, and some went to the scene of the massacre. They were among the first white people to see the mission after the fateful 29th of November 1847. What they saw must have sickened them. Everything that could be moved had been dragged into the buildings and burned. There were pieces of glass, china, pottery and iron strewn around the charred remains of the buildings. In Newell's own words, "papers, books, letters torn and many other things lay about the premises. Wagon wheels and other property had been placed in the house before it was burned. I got some letters and many laid about in the water."[42] To add to the horrible spectacle of debris and desolation the partially decayed bodies of those killed were lying about, having been disinterred by the wolves. Mrs. Victor tells of Joe Meek finding the body of his little daughter, Helen Mar Meek. It was no doubt a heart-breaking experience even to a tough old mountaineer like Joe Meek.[43] At this time some of

---

[40] Bancroft, op.cit., p. 711.

[41] Ibid., p. 715.

[42] Indian Wars, p. 179.

[43] Victor, River of the West, p. 233. Meek was on his way to Washington, D. C., with the memorial asking aid of Congress.

the party cut a lock from Mrs. Whitman's hair, which has been preserved in the Oregon Historical Society in Portland.[44]

The bodies of Dr. and Mrs. Whitman were reburied, "with a poling around them, nicely done," and the bodies of the rest were hastily placed in a common grave.[45]

The effect of this sight of death and destruction fired Gilliam with a determination to punish the Indians, peace commissioners notwithstanding. Newell confided to his diary that "The commissioners have no chance to arrange with the Indians, our supplies are short and our commander is quite hasty."[46] A fortification was started and preparations were made to fight even though it was known that Peu-Peu-mox-mox and a few Nez Perces were desirous to arrange peace negotiations.[47]

By the 6th of March it was known for certain that two hundred and fifty Nez Perces were approaching to join in peace talks at Waiilatpu. Many of the officers were willing to allow the commissioners to accomplish what they could, but Gilliam opposed such sentiment and threatened to go to battle the very day the Nez Perces were to arrive. Newell relates: "Colonel Gilliam left the council in a huff and declared he had come to fight and fight he would." This attitude further complicated the disciplinary problems in the army and Newell noted: "This army is composed of different kinds of men. Some have come to behave legally, others to plunder, and others for popularity. To do what we ought is easy if we could act together. Captain McKay and company deserve credit. In fact nearly all the officers seem to wish to do for the best."[48] Gilliam's threat to fight turned out to be only that, and on the 7th of March at Waiilatpu was held the great council, which the commissioners had so earnestly endeavored to accomplish.

---

[44] There is nothing to indicate who cut this lock of hair. Possibly it was Newell. He seems to have had a sense of value regarding perpetuation of the memory of unusual incidents as seen from his diaries. Tobie, op. cit., p. 155, states that Meek tucked away this lock of hair as a remembrance but he gives no authority for his statement. Victor, in River of the West, p. 433, does not give credit to Meek, but states: "Some tresses of golden hair were severed from the brow so terribly disfigured to be given to her friends in the Willamette as a last and only memorial."

[45] Newell Diary; Indian Wars, p. 179.

[46] Ibid.

[47] Bancroft, op.cit., p 717, footnote.

[48] Indian Wars, p. 181; Report of Commissioners.

According to the report of the commissioners, the following chiefs were present: the Walla Walla, Peu-Peu-mox-mox, a Cayuse war chief named Cashmashpello, and the Nez Perce chiefs, Joseph, Jacob, James, Red Wolf, Timothy, Richard, Kentuk, Luke, Stupetupenin Youmtama-laikin, Thomas and about two hundred and fifty warriors.[49]

> After the pipe of friendship had passed around till our hearts were all good and our eyes watery, we informed them that we had a communication for them from our head chief in the Willamette – and we wished them to break the seal which they did, and we read it to them, which called out the feelings of nearly all the chiefs the substance of the whole amounts to this; They had no knowledge of an intention on the part of the Cayuses to murder the Dr. till the deed was done. Then they heard it they were grieved, -- some of them came to see the chiefs, and inquire who had been guilty of so foul a deed – (They had a law amongst them) – that when one committed murder, he forfeited his own life – They had one head chief – they all listened to his words – Their old chiefs who were now dead had told them to be friendly with the Americans, and they had not forgotten their words – The Cayuses had told them the Americans were coming to kill all the Indians and to take their lands – but they still came on to see us – They had not killed Mr. Spalding but protected him – they ask him to stay with them – his property was still there, they would not join the murderers to fight us etc.[50]

General Palmer spoke first for the "head chief in the Willamette." He praised the Indians for their good conduct and warned them that the Cayuses had no more rights to their land because of their unlawful activity. All the white men asked of the

---

[49] Spectator, April 6, 1848.
[50] Ibid.

Nez Perces was a road through their territory. They would not settle on Nez Perce land without first obtaining their permission.[51]

Following Palmer, Newell in his slow, hesitating way, delivered a rather long speech to his friends, some of whom were his relatives by marriage. He was careful to point out his former relationship with all the Indians. Commending them warmly for their peaceful intentions, he added a warning that any other course might prove disastrous. The speech was a fine example of a common-sense appeal to the finer instincts of the savages, phrased in short, terse sentences which could easily be understood:

> Brothers: I have a few words to say, call together all your men, old and young, women and children. This day I am glad to see you here, we have come to talk with you and to tell you the duty we owe to our God and all good people. I have not come here to make peace with you, we never have been at war but always friendly. This I know, this all our people know. I have fought with the Nez Perces, some of them I see here, but we were on the same side; we have lost friends on the same day and at the same battle together. But we did not lose those friends in trying to kill innocent people, but by trying to save our own lives. This I have told our people, our people believe it. I have told them you are honest and good people, they believed it, your hands are not red with blood. I am glad, my children are glad – and now brothers hear me, never go to war with the Americans; if you do it will be your own fault and you are done. I have come here to see you. The Nez Perces and other good people, no one else. I am not here to fight but to separate the good from the bad, and to tell you that it is your duty to help make this ground clean. Thank God you have not helped to make it bloody. I was glad to hear the Nez Perces had no hand in killing Dr. Whitman, his wife and others. What have the Cayuses made, what have they lost. Everything,

---

[51] The full text of Palmer's speech may be found in the Spectator, April 6, 1848.

nothing left but a name. All the property they have taken in a short time will be gone, only one thing left, that is a name, the bloody Cayuses. They never will lose that only in this way, obey the great God and keep his laws. And, my friends, this must be done, if you will obey God and do what is right, we must. This is what our war chief has come for. What is our duty to the great God? This is his law. He who kills a man by man shall his blood be spilt. This is his law. This is what God says and he must be obeyed, or we have no peace in the land. There are good people enough here among the murders to have peace again in the land should they try. In a few days we could go about here as we have done, all friendly all happy. Will you hear or will you not. You have heard that we have come here to fight all the Indians, it is not so. The evil spirit has put bad words in the mouths of those murderers and they have told you lies.

My friends one thing more let me tell you; we have come here because it was our duty. We are sorry to have to come but the laws of God have been broken on this ground, look at these walls, see how black they are; look at that large grave. He is angry with those people who broke his laws and spilt innocent blood. How can we have peace? This way my friends and no other. All join together, and with good hearts try to get those murderers and do by them as the great God commands and by so doing, this land will be purified, and in no other way will we have peace. I am sorry to see people fight like dogs. People who love to kill and murder – they are bad people. We have come to get those murderers. If good men put themselves before those bad people, they are just as if they had helped to murder, and we will hold them as such. The most of the Cayuses have gone off but a few are here. They have left their farms. Why is this what have they done? Because some of their people have been foolish, all should not turn fools and be wicked. I

90

am sorry very sorry to see it so. What will they do if they fight us and fight against our God, and break our laws? I will tell you, they will become poor, no place will they find to hide their heads, no place on this earth nor a place in heaven, but down to hell should they go if Gods words are true. I hope you will be advised and take good council before it is too late.

Our war chiefs have waited a long time for the Cayuses to do what is right, he will wait no longer and when he begins to fight, I do not know when he will stop. His heart is so sore for Dr. Whitman and his wife, that have been slaves to this people, who done all they could to teach them how to work, and how to do all good things that they might live like the whites and be Christians, but they have joined the evil one and become bad; they have murdered they must not escape. My friends I am not angry, I am sorry. The other day over yonder where we fought the Cayuses, we saw people coming. I went with a flag I had no gun, made signs of peace, waved the flag for them not to shoot, but stop and talk, but they would not. I went back sorry, I knew there were some people there who had done us no harm, but those bad people told them lies and gave them horses to fight us. Bought them like slaves to fight. I knew they came blind, but they knew not what they were doing. I wanted to tell them what we had come for but could not. I have done my duty. God knows my heart. If I do wrong then the great God will punish me and now I tell you the same as if you were my own children. Do not join with those murderers nor let them come in your country or in your lodges, or eat with them, but try and bring them to justice.

My friends I have no more to say to you now. I have come a long way to see you and talk with you. Will you throw my words away? I hope not, I beg you to hear my words and be wise – I have brought this flag for the Nez Perces, take it I hope you will keep clear of blood. Let the Nez Perces assemble and settle among yourselves who will keep the flag. Ellis is not here, and many other chiefs are gone to the buffalo country that I am acquainted with. Mr. Craig will tell you that we are your friends, he loves you; so do we all like him; he has told us many good things of you.[52]

Lee and McKay spoke after Newell, substantiating the promises of the other speakers. After some social conversation, Palmer told the Indians that Mr. William Craig would remain with them for the present as his agent, "and would assist and instruct them in their efforts at agriculture."[53]

Newell then presented them with a large American flag, requesting that they preserve it and use it on all national occasions. The Indians received these tokens of friendship with "evident Good will" and after more friendly smoking, the Indians prepared to execute a war dance "which amused and delighted much, and we do them but bare justice when we say the performance was a well timed, the parts well acted, characters represented to the very life, and the whole first rate . . . We felt gratified with our success . . . in breaking the ranks of the enemy by calling off their allies and especially in separating the innocent from the guilty.[54]

Two days later another council was held with some of the Cayuses who consented to a talk. Colonel Gilliam, though he objected to the council in the first place and claimed that it was a scheme to gain time, offered to accept Joe Lewis in place of five murderers. This offer was rejected by the Indians, but it was obviously unjust to suggest freeing the guilty with but one exception. Newell wrote: "seeing such a move I concluded to be off." Another influential factor no doubt was his fear that some of the promises made to his Nez Perce friends would be broken by those of less responsibility in the army. The commissioners had

---

[52] Brown, op.cit., pp. 394-396. Also Spectator, April 6, 1848.
[53] Report of Commissioners. There is on file in Washington, D.C., a treaty in Lee's handwriting, which embodies the important agreements reached by the two parties. It is given in full in Brown, op.cit., p. 398. It was never signed.
[54] Report of Commissioners.

accomplished their work and concluded it was useless to continue with the army.

With no commissioners to restrain his aggressive nature, Colonel Gilliam took up the march in earnest, determined to capture the guilty Cayuses. The Indians succeeded in outwitting the army and escaped into the Palouse country, where they found a powerful ally in the Palouse Indians.

Nine days after the commissioners left, Colonel Gilliam was accidentally shot. While drawing a rope from a wagon his own gun was discharged into his body killing him instantly. His body arrived at Oregon City on April 6, the same day the commissioners' report was published in the Spectator.

The arrival of the peace commission at Oregon City received notice from the press:

> We stop the press to announce the return of Messrs. Newell and Palmer to this city. The commissioners and superintendent of Indian affairs have succeeded in securing the neutrality of the Nez Perces, Walla Walla and a small portion of the Cayuse and Yakimas. They also have intelligence upon which they confidently rely that the Spokanes, Flatheads and most of the upper country Indians are disposed to bear themselves friendly toward the whites.[55]

Thus ended the role of Newell as commissioner to the Indians. It seems most likely that had his advice been followed from the beginning, the war could have been entirely averted. Had the Indians been treated with pacific firmness rather than by war methods, the episode would have taken an entirely different course.

Newell was by no means a pacifist. When the desired results could not be gained peacefully he advised more severe methods. In a letter to James W. Nesmith in 1861 he advised erecting military posts in the Snake Indian region in Idaho and giving the Indians "a good thrashing" for their repeated misbehavior.[56]

The disagreement between Newell and Gilliam was inevitable. It has been noted that sending an army and a peace

---

[55] Spectator, March 23, 1848.
[56] Newell to Nesmith, January 13, 1861.

commission was in itself an apparent contradiction. The brutalities of the massacre had aroused the fighting spirit of the settlers, few of whom possessed the cool, common sense approach which Newell advocated. His former associations with the Indians gave him an appreciation of their position, something completely lacking in Gilliam. The revengeful fighting spirit of the settlers unfortunately found its epitome in Colonel Gilliam, and it may be wondered why Newell confided his accusations of petulance and impetuosity to his private diary. A man of Newell's political standing might well have aroused criticism of the Colonel's policies. There is no mention of any disagreement outside of Newell's private diary. No one can say what the outcome would have been had the commissioners not been appointed or Newell not been one of their number. It seems certain, however, that Newell's experience and knowledge of the Indians contributed in a very helpful way to the service performed by the commission.

For his services Newell received $66.70 six years later.[57]

---

[57] P. and T. Papers No. 1744. <u>Oregon Statesman</u>, November 28, 1854 (Hereafter cited <u>Statesman</u>).

CHAPTER VI

THE TERRITORY OF OREGON

After participating in the effort to make peace with the Indians, Newell returned to the Willamette Valley and resumed his active participation in the social and political life of the valley. In June 1848, he was reelected to the House of Representatives from the Champoeg district; in July he was chairman of "A Public Meeting of the Donors to the fund for supplying provisions to the distressed immigrants" held at the City hotel in Oregon City.[1]

When the legislature of 1848 convened in December, Dr. Newell did not appear. It is not evident just why he was not present, but his name is on the "list of the members who have resigned or left the territory."[2]   Whatever the reason, Newell's absence from public activity was short-lived. In August 1848, Congress officially made Oregon a territory,[3] and by the spring of 1849 the new territorial governor, Joseph Lane,[4] had arrived in Oregon City.

Among the problems that confronted Governor Lane were the unsettled Indian relations and the large exodus of Oregon's male population to the California gold mines. As soon as he had the legislative and judicial wheels running, while Joe Meek and his aides were taking the census and the elections were being held, Governor Lane was vigorously applying himself to the Indian problems, with the help of Robert Newell.

A short month after his arrival in March, Lane, an interpreter, and Robert Newell journeyed up the Columbia into the Cayuse country to communicate with the Indians and acquaint them with the intentions of the new government.[5]   Lane was returning

---

[1] Spectator, July 13, 1848.

[2] Oregon Archives, p. 258.

[3] For debates on the Oregon Question, see Congressional Globe, August 13, 1848, 30th Congress, 1st session.

[4] For a complete biography of Lane, see Sister Margaret Jean Kelly, Career of Joseph Lane, Frontier Politician (Washington, D.C.: the Catholic University of America Press, 1942).

[5] Statesman, March 28, 1854. This article indicates that Lane began negotiations with the Cayuses on this journey, which culminated in the surrender of five, who had been involved in the Whitman massacre.

Joseph Lane, First Territorial Governor of Oregon
Courtesy Salem Public Library. Salem, Oregon

from this expedition when he received word of disturbances among the Indians at Tumwater, and immediately set out for the Puget Sound area. Another message acquainted him with the arrival in the Columbia of the <u>Massachusetts</u>, with Captain Wood and troops aboard. With the news of the availability of troops the governor returned to the Columbia, where he found communications from the United States in regard to certain federal appointments, one of which concerned Newell.

In a letter to the Secretary of War, May 17, 1849, Governor Lane tells of Newell's appointment as Indian agent:

> But soon after my return about the middle of June I received instructions bearing date War Department office of Indian affairs August 31, 1848, also information of the appointment of J. Quinn Thornton, George C. Preston, and Robert Newell of Oregon, sub agents, to be employed and reside in that territory, and requiring the performance of certain duties therein specified . . . I promptly handed to Thornton and Newell their appointments.

They executed their bonds and took the oath required as will be seen by their bonds, which have been forwarded. Mr. Preston was then and is now absent from the territory and is supposed will not return. I therefore of necessity divided the territory into sub-agency districts and assigned J. Quinn Thornton to that part of the territory lying north of the Columbia River and Newell to the south of the Columbia, and on the 28th of June the above named sub-agents were furnished with their instructions....

Mr. Newell is an old mountaineer having spent ten years in the mountains where he followed trapping by which means he acquired a good knowledge of the tribes and their country. From 1839 to the present he has resided within the district to which he is assigned to duty[6] and has become well acquainted with the Indians in the valley of the Willamette – speaks tolerably well the tongues of several tribes and from his knowledge of the Indians and their country has made out and submitted his report from which I make such abstracts as in my opinion are of sufficient importance to entitle them to your consideration ....[7]

Newell's all around Indian knowledge made him a logical choice for his position. Probably no one in Oregon better understood the Indian problems or was better qualified to report on the existing conditions; but the gold fever that had attacked so many others in Oregon claimed Newell shortly after his appointment to the Indian agency.[8]

---

[6] This is an obvious error but of little significance. Newell arrived in Oregon in December 1840.

[7] House Executive Documents No. 1, 31st Congress, 2nd session, Series 595, pp. 156, 157.

[8] T. C. Elliott, op. cit., p. 118, states that Newell was appointed but did not qualify as Indian agent in 1849. Lane's letter is concrete proof that he not only qualified, but executed his bond and submitted at least one report.

Lane had reported that "nearly the entire male population of Oregon" went to the mines in forty-nine.[9] Farmers left their families, cattle and crops in the hope of "striking it rich" in California. Newell had considerable property to leave behind,[10] but the pull of the gold fields beckoned irresistibly.

A party of thirty men bound for California was organized with Newell as leader. The journey was enlivened by the danger of hostile Indians, and Newell proved to be an adequate captain in the fighting that was necessary before the party could proceed through the savage country. One of the skirmishes has been described by a contemporary who met Newell's party. At a particularly dangerous passage where the road was only wide enough for a wagon to pass, Newell noticed Indians hiding in the crevices of the rocks waiting to ambush the party. "With the capacity of a general he divided his

---

[9] Lane's observations give an interesting and informative picture of conditions then existing in Oregon. He wrote to the Secretary of State: "As soon as it was known in Oregon that gold in abundance could be obtained in California, many of the people left for the mines. Some have remained there, the most of them however have returned to see their families and spend the winter at home. But nearly all who have been there are now going back and most of them who have not been to the mines are also going . . . . In money the people are much benefitted. It is said and I suppose truly that at least one million of dollars in gold dust have been brought into Oregon; but on the other hand the country lately so productive and so capable of production, and which was rapidly being settled and being put into cultivation is now being neglected. Many are leaving their farms untenanted, many have failed to sow or put in crops of any kind, and many who have sowed will not harvest, consequently there will be but little produce. No improvements are being made, not a house is being put up – fine saw and grist mills on never failing streams are standing still for want of laborers, a large portion of the horses and cows are being taken to the mines for sale – labor and subsistence is exorbitantly high . . . ." Senate Executive Documents No. 52, 31st Congress, 1st session, Vol. 13.
[10] The census report of 1850 showed that Newell had 540 acres of unimproved land, 100 acres of improved land, 20 swine, 3 working oxen, 25 milk cows, forty other cattle, farm machinery valued at $150 and 100 bushels of Irish potatoes. The farm was valued at $6,000. United States Census Schedule 1 Report for Marion County 1850, Government Report on Production of Agriculture in Marion County Territory of Oregon 1850 Oregon State Library, Salem.

forces as to command the situation."[11] Part of his men were dispatched to act as a decoy along the road to draw the fire of the Indians, yet so situated as not to be in danger. A small group was stationed in ambush as a reserve while the remainder was ordered to circle the Indians until the dense cover of wild plum bushes was reached, whereupon the men were to creep up into the midst of the Indians and shoot them down. This maneuver was intended to confuse the savages and was executed with amazing success. The Indians were being shot down before they were aware of the whites being among them. Those who had drawn the attention of the Indians blocked an escape in front. The reserves protected the rear, which left only one possible avenue of retreat along the face of the bluff. At the opportune moment another party led by Weston and Howard came from the south, and hearing the shots, hurried forward to ascertain the cause of the commotion. At the sight of the savages fleeing from the rocks the party opened fire on the Indians. This event completely routed the latter, and leaving themselves completely unprotected, the Indians jumped into a river in an attempt to reach the sheltering forest on the other side. "The miners continued their firing until the river ran red. The slaughter must have been very great."[12]

Newell evidently did not find gold in sufficient quantities to warrant his remaining in California,[13] for he was back in Oregon with his family in 1850.[14] His stay was long enough, however, to lose him the position of Indian agent. Samuel R. Thurston, a Democrat and Oregon's first delegate to Congress, secured Newell's removal. The entry in his diary for December 11, 1849, reads:

> This morning I called on Secretary of the Interior
> Thos. Ewing to find out what instructions had been

---

[11] "Reminiscences of William M. Case," O.H.Q. (September 1900), I:293. Case was leading a party from California to Oregon when he met Newell's group.

[12] Ibid., p. 294.

[13] The writer has been unable to find further information pertaining to Newell's stay in California. The dates of the journey are not known at this time.

[14] The children living with the family in 1850, as enumerated by the census of that year, were: Rebecca, Thomas, Francis, William, Marquis, and Robert. United States Census for 1850, typed copy, Marion County Census, Oregon Historical Society.

given to the Governor of Oregon relative to Indian affairs. The secretary sent me to the chief clerk of the Indian bureau for this information. I then brought to his notice Robert Newell, sub-Ind. agent in Oregon requesting his removal. He informed me to write him a letter on the subject and he would attend to it . . . .

On December 29 Thurston made another short entry: "This morning I went to see the Sec. of the Interior. He informed me that he had removed R. Newell and appointed J. L. Parrish."[15]

The year 1850 brought a change in government officers in Oregon. With the election of Taylor came a Whig administration and a new governor for the territory.[16] Lane had served Oregon well in his short term as head of the government, and had gained the admiration and respect of Oregon citizens for his aggressive administration. His Whig successor, John P. Gaines, arrived in Oregon with the pomp and ceremony of an aristocrat, and from his first appearance evinced a temperament entirely different from that of the energetic Lane. Then too, Lane had become a familiar and popular figure and was a staunch Democrat, a fact pleasing to the settlers, who were themselves primarily Democratic at this time.[17] They were satisfied with Lane, and the fastidious, grandiloquent Gaines, careful to guard his dignity, precipitated an era of bitter partisan strife.

Newell was an active participant in the political battles of the fifties, though he was no longer a member of the legislature. With the increase in population brought about by the large immigrations, Newell found determined opposition to his candidacy as representative from Marion County. He was elected without exception from 1843 to 1849, but at the regular June election in

---

[15] "Diary of Samuel Royal Thurston," O.H.Q. (September, 1914), XV:162. Presumably Newell was removed because he had left the office to go to California, though Newell implied that it was due to the change in administration.

[16] Lane's last act as governor was to sign the death warrants of the five Indians accused of complicity in the Whitman massacre. See Bancroft, op. cit., II:93-100.

[17] Woodward, op. cit., pp. 37-57.

1850, Newell was sixth in a field of eight candidates.[18]   At the special election in November of 1850 he received 92 votes for "member of the house of representatives," but Benjamin F. Harding received 128 votes and was elected.[19]   These defeats were quite convincing setbacks and Newell was not a candidate again until 1854.

Artist sketch of the Oregon Statehouse, Oregon City, Oregon 1849
Reprinted with Permission from the Statesman Journal
Courtesy of the Salem Public Library Photo Collection, Salem, Oregon

Despite his legislative defeats Newell took an active part in the capital location controversy, a troublesome question since Oregon's earliest governmental proceedings. The problem came up again in the legislative session beginning December 2, 1850. The principal towns involved were Oregon City, where the legislature was then convening, and Salem.   Prominent among those advocating Salem was Asahel Bush, who later engaged in a squabble with Newell over the capital issue.[20] The discussion in the

---

[18] Original Report of voting in Marion County November 25, 1850. In the handwriting of I. M. Gilbert, clerk, Oregon Historical Society, MS 1824.
[19] Ibid., MS 1833.
[20] Asahel Bush came to Oregon for the express purpose of editing a newspaper which was to further the political interests of Samuel Thurston.

101

legislature of 1850-51 culminated in "An Act to provide for the selection of places for location and erection of the public buildings of the Territory of Oregon."[21] This act not only located the capital at Salem, it authorized the erection of a penitentiary at Portland and the building of a university at Marysville (now Corvallis). While the bill was being discussed in legislature, Governor Gaines sent a message criticizing the bill and stating that the Congressional act creating the Territory of Oregon explicitly forbade any law, which embraced more than one object. "To avoid improper influences, which may result from intermixing in one and the same act such things as have no proper relation to each other every law shall embrace but one object, and that shall be expressed in the title."[22] The legislature, which disliked Gaines and his politics,[23] passed the bill without changing its form to comply with Gaines' request.[24] The bill helped to crystallize a line of demarcation between the Democrats and the Whigs, although there were some in each party who favored still other locations.

With the appearance of the Oregon Statesman, a Democratic weekly edited by Asahel Bush, a new era in Oregon politics was begun. Bush worked for a tighter and more effective Democratic organization, using the Statesman as an effective aid. "Through its editor, Asahel Bush, cold calculating, and relentless, it was to dominate Oregon politics for a decade, making and breaking politicians at will."[25] Newell was a Democrat as well as Bush, but the two men were diametrically opposed on the bill locating the capital.

The question of the legality of the capital location act was finally left to the decision of the justices of the supreme court of

---

Though his paper was first established in Oregon City, Bush actively supported the Salem group in the Capital controversy. See Turnbull, op. cit., p. 80.

[21] Statutes of a General Nature Passed by the Legislative Assembly of the Territory of Oregon (Oregon City: Asahel Bush, Printer, 1851), (Hereafter cited General Laws.)

[22] General Laws, p. 40.

[23] See Statesman, March 28, 1851. This was the first issue. The first Whig paper was the Weekly Oregonian, issued first in December 1850, and edited by Thomas J. Dryer. For Dryer's sentiments on the capital issue see Oregonian, December 6, 1851.

[24] The vote was 16 to 11. Bancroft, op. cit., II:146.

[25] Woodward, op. cit., p. 40.

Oregon. But a difficulty immediately arose, for where were the judges to convene, at Salem or at Oregon City? The two Whig judges, Chief Justice Thomas Nelson and Justice William Strong, ruled that the location bill violated section six of the territorial act and was therefore illegal, leaving Oregon City the legal seat of the government.[26]

The majority of the legislature favored Salem, and encouraged by the lone Democrat on the supreme court bench, Judge O. C. Pratt, convened at Salem on December 1, 1851.[27] The split among the justices and the defiance of the legislature intensified the partisan nature of the controversy and fanned the flames of political animosity. Governor Gaines staunchly maintained his stand. When the United States attorney general evaded a ruling on the legality of the act requested by Gaines, the Governor, the other federal officers, and the two Whig justices remained at Oregon City, while the legislature met at Salem.

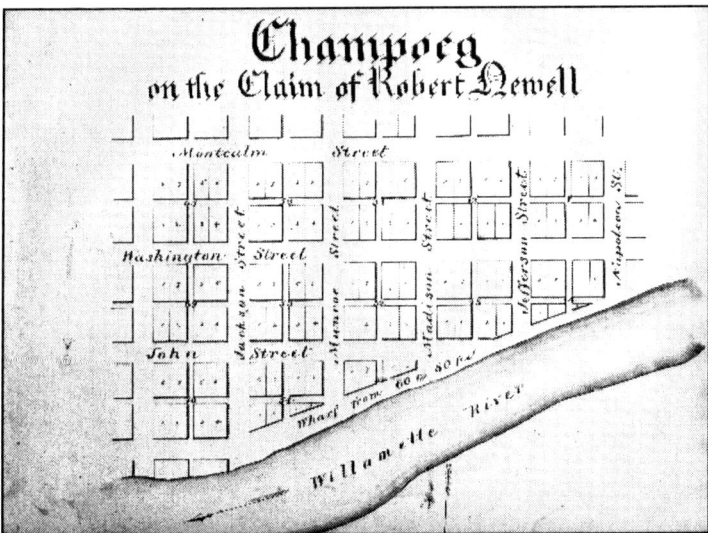

Platt Map for the portion of Champoeg that sat on Robert Newell's Donation Land Claim
Courtesy Champoeg State Heritage Area, Champoeg, Oregon

---

[26] See <u>House Executive Documents No. 104</u>, 32nd Congress, 1st session, Series No. 648 (Article 3), pp. 7-24. Strong's opinion: "It is my opinion that Oregon City is at this time the legal seat of government."
[27] Charles Henry Carey, <u>The Oregon Constitution and Proceedings and Debate of the Constitutional Convention of 1857</u> (Salem, Oregon: State Printing Dept., 1926), p. 9.

In the meantime, in July of 1851, Newell became postmaster at Champoeg, and in October of the same year he opened a general store there. The combination of post office and general store with his farm proved to be a lucrative one. He advertised his store in the Spectator, October 28, 1851:

Store at Champoeg
The undersigned has a very good assortment of Goods and Groceries for the farming community which he will exchange for wheat, oayts, hides, pork, butter, chickens, eggs or cash. Call anyhow and see if you have letters in the post office.
Robert Newell.

Newell's offer to donate land in Champoeg for the location of the capital has been mentioned. Since Champoeg was closer to Oregon City than Salem, it was to his financial advantage to have the capital continue in its first location.

With a deadlock between the two groups of governing officials, the public began to speak its mind. Newell was chairman of a meeting at Champoeg on December 25, 1851, which gathered "for the purpose of getting an expression of public opinion in reference to the course of our federal officers and the proceedings of the members elect to our present territorial assembly."[28] The group strongly denounced the activity of the legislature in disregarding the decision of the supreme court outlawing Salem as the seat of government. They adopted a resolution to abide by the decision of Judges Nelson and Strong and severely castigated Judge Pratt for his "meddlesome course through the public journals and otherwise," by which he encouraged the people and the representatives to disobey the supreme law of the land.

In a speech at this meeting Newell criticized the "Salemites" for their selfish motives and disregard of authority. Whatever his reasons for adopting the Oregon City position, Newell found himself under the handicap of being a Democrat advocating what was regarded as a Whig position. Editor Bush was quick to perceive the opportunity and loosed a bolt of Democratic lightning

---

[28] Statesman, December 30, 1851.

against him in the same issue of the Statesman, which contained the transactions of the Champoeg public meeting:

> This "meeting" was devised and directed by the cabal of federal officers in Oregon City . . . Robert Newell, the chairman of this meeting and the proprietor of the embryo town where it was held (Champoeg) is in this instance the cats paw with which they haul their chestnuts from the fire. A pretended Democrat he has ever been the fawning sycophant and obedient servant of the junto of Whig federal officers in this city who are prompted by party and other considerations . . . . He belongs to the men he serves – they have bought him for a price and with a statement of consideration we leave him to their control and them to enjoy the fruits of their purchase . . . He enjoys the smiles and the dirty work of Washington federalism and the value of his purchased opinion is not hard to estimate . . . . [29]

Bush enumerated the instances when Newell had accepted money from a Whig government for services he had never performed, and charged that Newell had sent a friend to Washington with the avowed purpose of securing his appointment as Indian agent. If Newell had, he had only successfully accomplished what many other office-seekers in the Territory tried to do.

Newell answered Bush's accusations and surprisingly enough, Bush published the letter in the Statesman:

> You say the commissioners hired me at five dollars per day for many months service I never performed. That assertion Mr. Bush is untrue as the rest of your comments and I can prove it, but to contradict you flat in my opinion is only an inducement for you to belch forth from your paper volumes of scurility.
>
> The truth is in my opinion Mr. Bush that you did not nor do not now believe what you have written

---

[29] Ibid.

about me . . . . I think you have done it to forstall public opinion and taken this unfair course to accomplish your designe: As to my politics if you wished to be honest just why did you not say that I had been appointed Indian sub-agent by James K. Polk, President of the United States, and had been moved out by the present administration.[30] Why if you wished to be fair, did you not inform the public that when Governor Lane came here as superintendent of Indian affairs I was the only one that came and went and assisted in every way I could as sub-agent to assist him in his official duties, he was a government officer I thought to serve him was doing my duty but according to your doctrine I should have disowned him, but that course I did not take, but supported him throughout and at the last call I was up and doing, and at the close of the day our ballot boxe gave in our precinct one against 17 or over for Joe Lane . . . .

Newell continues with a blistering attack on Bush, charging him with advocating "Mormonish" policies and "trying to run the officers of old Uncle Sam out of the country."[31]

Newell's friendship with Lane was apparent while Lane was in Oregon and continued after he had been elected Delegate to Congress replacing Thurston.[32]

Newell wrote to Lane while the latter was in Washington, and judging by the general tone of his letters he expected Lane to go along with the decision of Judges Nelson and Strong, although he admitted he was somewhat confused. "Things is so mixed up and crosswise that it has got beyond the comprehension of any mountain man I ever saw."[33] Lane had intimated friendship to the Whigs as

---

[30] Newell was removed by Thurston, an avowed Democrat. The statement by Newell that the change of administrations caused his removal does not appear to be valid.

[31] Statesman, January 6, 1852.

[32] Lane had been nominated to replace Thurston before the latter returned from Congress. Both were Democrats and a possible split in the party over the two was prevented by the sudden death of Thurston. See Statesman, May 2, 1851.

[33] Newell to Lane, February 1, 1852. Oregon Historical Society.

well as the Democrats. Some of the correspondence of the period shows the disgust of a few of the strong Democrats at Lane's bi-partisan policies. Bush received a letter from Reuben P. Boise explaining the dissatisfaction in Portland because Lane "is entirely noncommittal and trying to shave every question that is asked."[34] Matthew P. Deady, one of the promising young Democrats in Oregon, wrote to Bush: "I wish Lane could shake off these Whig politicians from his skirts. If not, the day will come when he will regret it and the Democratic party also."[35]

Whether Whig or Democrat, those who supported Lane were soon to be reminded with abruptness that Lane had decided to cast his lot with the Salemites, and the majority of the Democrats. Deady had offered a resolution authorizing a memorial to Congress which the legislature had accepted, "in view of the action of Nelson and Strong."[36] This memorial was sent to Lane, who reported what he had done in a letter to Bush:

> . . . In regard to the location of the seat of government and the proceedings of the Legislative Assembly at Salem, I will also state that sometime since, I introduced a Joint Resolution approving and confirming the act of the Assembly location the Seat of Government at Salem and also approving the proceedings of the Legislative Assembly at Salem. This Joint Resolution will, I have no doubt, pass and will, I hope, settle the Seat of Gov't., and the lawfulness of the proceedings of the assembly at their late session at Salem are concerned.[37]

Either Newell did not know that Lane sympathized with the Salemites or he was endeavoring to change the Delegate's ideas on the matter, for he wrote:

---

[34] Boise to Bush, May 1, 1851. University of Oregon Library.

[35] Deady to Bush, May 4, 1851. University of Oregon Library.

[36] Full text of the memorial, Journal of the House of Representatives, Oregon Legislature (Hereafter cited Journal of the House) December 1, 1851, Appendix, pp. 1-6.

[37] This letter dated March 21, 1852, is unsigned but apparently written by Lane for the author calls himself a representative of the people. Naseeb M. Malouf, Asahel Bush, Unpublished thesis, University of Oregon History Department.

Bush has cut loose and has and will say anything
that he thinks will go down with the people, he legs
for Pratt and no doubt intends Pratt, as many others
do, to take your place as delegate when your time is
up but by the Eternal that never will happen in my
opinion. I am sorry to say the Democratic party has
somewhat split here, I cannot believe the honest
Democracy will ever sanction the conduct of those
Salemites, neither do I believe they will last long.[38]

This sounds a little as though Newell was endeavoring to frighten
Lane into leaving Bush and the Salemites by suggesting Bush was
backing Pratt for Lane's position – a thought Bush may have
considered and discarded because of Lane's popularity. Though
Newell was correct in his statement regarding the split in the
Democratic Party, he was sadly lacking in political perspicacity in
his prediction that the Salem faction or "clique" would soon
disappear. Bush and his fellow Salemites became the very heart of
the Democratic Party in Oregon, [39] and their first big achievement
was the settlement of the capital controversy as they had planned,
even though in so doing they split the party-line wheat from the
more individualistic Democratic chaff.

The capital issue furnished a pretense to start an organized
Democratic party, though not all Democrats were convinced of the
wisdom of the move. Most of the legislature was Democratic, and
most of the citizens of Oregon resented the Whig officers appointed
to govern the Territory. While the legislature met at Salem, the
federal officers maintained their position at Oregon City, so that
though Bush did not "consider it the capital location controversy
exactly a political matter, yet the parties concerned necessarily make
it somewhat so, especially if we look ahead a few years."[40] By
emphasizing the representative position held by the Legislative
Assembly and the appointive position of the federal (Whig) officers,
Bush cleverly gained support for the Democratic position.

As the controversy continued the newspapers became more
vitriolic. Dryer poured out the wrath of the Whigs by his editorials

---

[38] Newell to Lane, February 1, 1852.
[39] Woodward, op. cit., pp. 40-41.
[40] Quoted by Woodward, op. cit., p. 45.

in the Oregonian, scourging Bush and his adroit efforts to consolidate his organization of the Democratic Party. Said Dryer: "The vice-president of the association of gentlemen – proprietor and principal editor of the late "vox populi" – ought to have a medal manufactured out of Skunk's eyes, for his services in Oregon."[41]

Again in April 1852, Newell informed Lane of the continued dishonesty of "those scamps" in Salem. He informed Lane that Bush in his opinion would "fail here and some honorable Democrat take his place."

Newell thought that Deady's memorial to Congress would fall flat: "The people in time will see too well the design of Deady by presenting such a memorial I never have thought nor do I now, that it will pass the Senate or even the House . . . . We have enough of trouble now but let that be passed and trouble and confusion with poverty would no doubt exist."[42]

There was reason for the Whigs and a few opposing Democrats to suppose that the decision of Judges Nelson and Strong would finally be vindicated. President Fillmore was advised of the situation through the treasury department, who wished to know how to appropriate money for the erection of the buildings when there was no agreement as to where the buildings were to be located. The Attorney General, J. J. Crittenden, finally gave an opinion on the case, ruling that:

> . . . the act is too explicit to leave room for construction . . . . By the force of this language the governor must have concurrent and equal power with the Assembly not only in the application of this money to the erection of the necessary buildings, but in the selection of the place where they are to be erected . . . .
>
> My opinion, therefore, of the act in question is, that it is null and void in all its parts, and consequently can give no legal validity to anything done under color of its authority.[43]

---

[41] Oregonian, February 14, 1852.
[42] Newell to Lane, April 10, 1852, Oregon Historical Society.
[43] House Executive Documents No. 104, 32nd Congress, 1st session (Article 2), pp. 6-7.

Regardless of this decision, the legislature continued to meet at Salem. As the argument gained heat, Judge Nelson threatened to resign. Again the citizens around Champoeg called a meeting to register their protest against the editor of the Oregon Statesman and his "aspiring associates," and to publicly express appreciation to Judge Nelson who "at the earnest solicitation of many of our citizens, determined to withhold his contemplated resignation."[44] At this meeting Newell was selected one of a committee of ten to prepare resolutions to be submitted to the Oregonian, the Democratic Times and the Spectator. Whether or not these public meetings brought pressure to bear on the legislature, they did make known public feeling, and provided the main outlet for political activity for those who were not a part of the legislative body.

Oregon City Democrats and Whigs alike protested the party line being drawn solely on the location issue. Those who had property to consider were forced to take sides irrespective of party allegiance. In April the people around Clackamas and Oregon City gathered to discuss the political situation. A resolution deprecating the existing policy of drawing party lines in Oregon was adopted unanimously.[45] Judge Buck, a Democrat, spoke at this meeting and opposed the attempt being made to organize the Democratic party in Oregon upon the basis of local issues and personal antipathies. All these meetings around Oregon City naturally emphasized the lawless character of the Legislative assembly and vehemently protested "the doctrine that a majority of the members elect to the legislative assembly, finding themselves together in the Rogue river mines, or in Bear river valley, or upon a hunting frolick, or upon a pleasure excursion or in an Indian Campaign, may there make, alter or repeal laws in the character of the legislative assembly."[46] As the quarrel continued, newspaper editorials became more and more picturesque in language.

Though the Whigs hoped the split in the Democratic party would hamper the Democrats at the polls, it proved to be of minor

---

[44] Spectator, March 16, 1852.
[45] Oregonian, May 8, 1852.
[46] Ibid.

significance in the elections of June 1852. The Democrats secured a convincing majority.[47]

The location problem was officially settled in April of 1852 by a Congressional joint resolution passed by the House on April 26 and by the Senate on April 27. The announcement of the decision by the two opposing newspapers makes an interesting study. The Statesman in bold type crowed:

> The question settled; The people, the Legislative assembly and Judge Pratt sustained; the Whig Federal Officers Rebuked and Condemned; Nelson's and Strong's Assumed "Supreme Court" Unrecognized and Upset Order Restored to Oregon . . . .

> So unquestionably right have been the people, and so grossly wrong the Whig Federal Officers that no one man in either branch could be found to oppose the former and uphold the latter . . . . Never was the triumph of right and correct principles more perfect, and never was the overthrow of error and misrule more complete.[48]

A Sketch of Salem in mid 1800's
Courtesy of Salem Public Library, Salem, Oregon

---

[47] Woodward, op. cit., p. 50.
[48] Statesman, June 29, 1852.

The article commended Lane for his efforts in securing the passage of the resolution, a note that must have perturbed Newell and others who had depended on Lane to uphold the decision of Nelson and Strong. Nine years later Newell wrote to Nesmith: "I must confess that I have a little desire to be avenged for the course that old Joe Lane took in Oregon."[49]

The Oregonian published a long article in which Dryer gave his reasons for opposing the location act, and rather plaintively remarked that further discussion could not alter the result. Dryer was determined to abide by the laws "by observing and upholding their mandates" as well as "by denouncing their transgression."[50] Dryer left for a future decision whether Lane "had not pandered to the schemes of faction, and whether his action has not tended to build upon the ruins of law and order and good government a band of conspirators against the peace and order of the people."[51]

So ended the capital location controversy, although in the hearts of many the question remained unsettled. Newell had been actively engaged in an attempt to locate the capital, first in Champoeg while he was a legislator, then at Oregon City when his participation in the conflict was carried on as an ordinary citizen. Though he applied himself assiduously, his efforts were in vain.

With the close of the location question, Newell's political activity decreased, though he was active in several financial adventures in 1854.[52] The Statesman of April 4, 1854, reports that he was one of the commissioners "under the direction of a majority of whom subscriptions may be received to the capital stock of the Oregon California Railroad Company hereby incorporated." But the company was unversed in the methods of finance necessary to construct and operate a railroad enterprise, and nothing came of this early attempt.[53]

---

[49] Newell to Nesmith, January 13, 1861.

[50] Oregonian, June 26, 1852.

[51] Ibid.

[52] The only record of political activity until the late 1850's appears in precinct report of Marion County of 1854. When Newell received only five votes for constable, his opponent, Mr. Mason, received 55. Oregon Historical Society, MS 199.5.

[53] See Lyman, op. cit., IV:261. For a history of early railroads see Joseph Gaston, "Genesis of The Oregon Railway System," O.H.Q. (June, 1906), VII:105-107.

To add to his duties as postmaster and general storekeeper, Newell completed the building of a large flourmill at Champoeg in April of 1855. "It is capable of turning out a large quantity of flour and those who have used samples of it say it is of very superior quality."[54] In those days Champoeg was the outlet for the most extensive wheat growing county in Oregon. The Statesman continued: We believe it the best place in Oregon for a large establishment like Dr. Newell's."[55]

The outbreak of Indian hostilities in Oregon and Washington in 1855 prompted Newell to organize a select group of fifty scouts. These men were well acquainted with the country and some of them were old trapping friends of Newell.[56] The company was accepted into the Service of the United States with Robert Newell as Captain and commander. Their activity was restricted to the area west of Walla Walla, perhaps because Newell feared an excursion east of this region would necessitate a fight with the Nez Perces who were his friends and relatives by marriage.[57] The company was disbanded by General Wool in January 1856, after serving four months.[58] Though the records do not indicate the exact nature of the service performed, Newell was recommended favorably to the government for his activity in the war of 1855-56.[59]

Following his war service, Newell apparently contented himself with his many duties at Champoeg until 1858, when he entered again into politics, this time, as before, in the ranks of the Democratic party. He was defeated in June by J. W. Grim and E. F. Colby in a bid for election to the House of Representatives in the Oregon Legislature.[60]

The following year in March he was elected chairman of the Marion County Democratic convention and chosen delegate to represent the county at the State Democratic convention held in Salem.[61]

---

[54] Statesman, April 10, 1855.
[55] Ibid.
[56] Evans, op. cit. p. 541. Elliott, op. cit., p. 119. The author has been unable to locate Newell's name among the Muster Rolls given by Victor in Early Indian Wars. Elliott states that Newell served under Major Rains.
[57] Elliott, op. cit., p. 119.
[58] Evans, op. cit. p. 549.
[59] Statesman, May 1, 1860.
[60] Statesman, June 22, 1858.
[61] Statesman, March 29, 1859.

In the same year Newell became the first grand master of the Champoeg Masonic Lodge No. 27. He held this position for three years.[62]

Eighteen fifty-nine brought an end to the long agitation for statehood and Oregon became a state on February 14. Sixteen years after Newell and his mountain friends supported the American cause at the organization meeting in Champoeg, Oregon had become a full-fledged part of the union. Thus ended the arduous labor of those who would not be satisfied with a government separate from the United States or dominated by any other nation. They had overcome the greatest hardships to make their way to Oregon. Though at first they were outnumbered by those favoring British allegiance, these pioneers stood firm against all who opposed citizenship in the United States. To achieve their goal the settlers were forced to fight an Indian war, and to deal with the savages under extremely dangerous conditions. The relentless push of the pioneers from the east, with the resultant expanding frontier, meant more people in Oregon to exploit her resources. These immigrations were encouraged by liberal land laws so that by 1856 the population was estimated to be over 35,000.[63] The inhabitants of Oregon had every reason to look back at their history with pride and to look ahead with optimism after they entered the union February 14, 1859.

---

[62] Original Minutes of Champoeg Lodge, No. 27. The lodge is now located at Canby. The writer talked with several of the lodge members and was shown the original minutes of 1859. In the lodge hall is a large picture of Newell with the dates of his incumbency. Many of the records of the lodge were lost in the flood of 1861, when the lodge building was moved several miles down river by the high water.

[63] For a complete discussion of Oregon's rise to Statehood, see R. C. Clark, History of the Willamette Valley, Oregon (Chicago: S. D. Clarke Publishing Co., 1927, Chapters X and XIV; Carey, op. cit., pp. 466-520; Lyman, op. cit., Vol. III. A good book on the importance of the West as a whole, Dan Elbert Clark, The West In American History (New York: Thomas Y. Crowell, 1937).

CHAPTER VII

PUBLIC CAREER AND PERSONAL LOSS
1860-1861

The year 1860 brought Newell's election to the state legislature. But before he resumed the legislative position he participated in an experiment, which sought to defray the expenses of the state penitentiary, at that time located in Portland. The existing buildings were inadequate to keep the convicts in proper quarters or assure their confinement until their sentences had been served.

Portland as seen in 1857
From the Ben Maxwell Collection
Courtesy of Salem Public Library, Salem, Oregon

Lessee of the Penitentiary

The Legislature of 1856-57 had abolished the "Board of Building Commissioners" and placed in its stead a superintendent[1] who was given power to make all authorized improvements, alterations and repairs on the building and "to appoint some suitable

---

[1] General Laws 1856-1857, pp. 9, 10.

and discreet person whose duty it shall be to keep, feed and take care of any and all convicts which are now or hereafter confined in the penitentiary."[2]

The duties outlined above were assigned to Joseph Sloan.[3] The legislature had given authority to the superintendent to use the convicts to make bricks and cut building stones, which were to be sold at market price. By this arrangement, it was thought, the expenses of keeping the jail could be considerably lowered.

For several reasons this set-up proved unworkable. The number of convicts doubled during the first year. Such a large increase necessitated enlarging the existing facilities. The superintendent was empowered to advertise for sealed bids for a sufficient quantity of stone to construct fourteen additional cells. When the bids were opened, they proved too high to be practical, and the superintendent refused to let the contract which he contended would have cost the Territory $7,300 over the cost of building the same cells with brick.[4]

The superintendent decided against the propriety of brick making on the grounds of the penitentiary. The grounds were inadequate and the staff of supervisors too small to allow the convicts to work in a brick yard. Brick making required night work and the chance of escape at night would be increased. Since the necessary funds to begin such an operation were not available, nothing in the way of building was done. The increase in the number of inmates required an increased supervisory staff and an increase in the money necessary to provide board for the convicts. With no bricks forthcoming, the funds had to be paid by the territorial government. The superintendent was forced to use money from his personal account to defray the expense of extra clothing, bedding, and kitchen equipment necessitated by the increase in prisoners.[5]

---

[2] Ibid., p. 11.

[3] General Laws, 1858-1859, Appendix, p. 54. The appointment of the superintendent was left to the Governor. See General Laws 1856-1857, p. 9.

[4] General Laws 1858-1859, Appendix, p. 55. Report of the Superintendent of jail to the Legislature.

[5] Ibid. The legislature passed a law which punished by death those convicts "who with a deadly weapon shall strike, wound, stab, shoot or shoot at" those having lawful charge for them. Statesman, February 16, 1858.

The Legislature of 1858-59 passed a law which changed the name of the officer in charge of the penitentiary from superintendent to inspector and made the office elective. The law entitled "an act to more effectually provide for the Labor and Safe keeping of the Penitentiary convicts"[6] sought to remedy the faults of the previous act by providing for the leasing of the penitentiary. "The inspector shall have power to farm out the penitentiary and the convict labor thereof to the best responsible bidder for a term of not less than three nor more than five years."[7] Lessees were required to give bond for thirty thousand dollars.

Several propositions were submitted to the Legislative Assembly in 1859,[8] but the final bill passed leased the penitentiary and the convict labor to Robert Newell and L. N. English.[9]

The Statesman noted the plan on June 21, 1859, after the bill passed the Senate:

> A bill has passed the Senate leasing L. N. English and Robert Newell the State prison at Portland and all tools etc. appertaining there to, together with the convicts for a period of five years. The consideration is that the lessees shall maintain the said convicts without cost to the state for the labor they perform . . . . If successful and we do not see why it may not so prove, will save the State many thousands of dollars. Messers. Newell and English took possession of the penitentiary and convicts the 22 inst. in pursuance of the law . . . . There were thirty-one convicts. They are employing them in grading the streets of Portland.

The law repealed the former provision providing an inspector of the penitentiary while the lessees were faithfully carrying out their part of the agreement; if they should fail in their

---

[6] General Laws 1858-1859, p. 35.

[7] Ibid., p. 36.

[8] General Laws 1858-1859, Appendix, pp. 77, 88.

[9] The bill was amended many times. Discussion on the bill can be found in the proceedings of the so-called extra session of 1859, pp. 36, 50, 57, 68, 74, 75, 77, 78, 79, 80, 81. The final passage occurred June 2, 1859.

duties or abandon their lease, the governor was given power to appoint an inspector.

Convicts working outside of the prison walls proved to be a menace. Escapes were frequent and criticism resulted.

> Another convict named Punkerton escaped from the penitentiary a few days since. The lessee offers a reward of $150 for his rendition. The penitentiary as at present conducted is a humbug, a nuisance and a curse to the community, and the sooner a change is made in its management the better. There are now several convicts at large, reckless and desparate outlaws forced to subsist by robbery and violence . . . .[10]

Newell and English sublet the penitentiary to Robert Pentland, Stephen Coffin, and L. Besser within a few months after they had acquired the lease, perhaps because they saw the impossibility of profitably employing the prisoners due to the many officers necessary to prevent the more desperate from escaping.

When the legislature convened in 1860 a special committee was appointed to consider the problem. Newell was present in the House as a Democrat from Marion County and was a member of this committee.[11] The matter was finally settled in 1862 when the legislature prohibited the working of convicts away from the prison, in response to a request from the Governor.[12]

---

[10] Statesman, March 6, 1860. There is a very exhaustive report on the penitentiary in Biennial Message of Gov. L. F. Grover, to the Legislative Assembly of the State of Oregon. Eighth session 1874 (Salem: Mart V. Brown, state printer, 1874), pp. 1-69. The author has been unable to establish the date Newell and English sub-let the penitentiary. There is an article in the Statesman of September 20, 1859, which states that Coffin and Pentland had trouble in keeping the convicts confined. Presumably they were in charge for three months at the most. In that case they were not in charge when the criticism became vehement after January of 1860.
[11] Journal of the House, September 11, 1860. Also Statesman, September 18, 1860.
[12] The experiment of leasing out the penitentiary did solve the pecuniary problem because the state was not financially obligated. The citizens of Portland, however, objected because of the large number of escapees and because the convict labor around the city provided competition to the "free

Democratic Member of the Legislature

When the Marion County Democratic Convention met on the 14th of April 1860, Robert Newell, as in 1859, was in the chair. He was nominated to run for the House of Representatives with B. F. Harding, Samuel Parker, and C. P. Crandall. Presumably Newell's attitude toward slavery was at one with that of the county convention, which repudiated the doctrine that Congress should be given the power to "interfere with the institution of slavery in the Territories of the United States, either to establish, protect or prohibit the same." Marion County Democrats protested the Congressional position of their Senators, for Congress had been in favor of protection of slavery in the territories. Such convictions were obviously in harmony with the principles enunciated by Stephen A. Douglas and the convention adopted another resolution stating their preference for Douglas as a candidate for President.[13]

After being elected for the first time since 1848,[14] Newell, with his fellow Democrats of Marion County, Samuel Parker, C. P. Crandall and B. F. Harding, met with the House of Representatives at the first regular meeting on September 10, 1860.[15]

Newell was a member of the committee on Indian affairs,[16] as well as that appointed to consider the problems arising from the lease of the penitentiary.[17] As chairman of the last-named committee, he recommended to the House that a committee be appointed to visit the jail and report to the House conditions there. The committee duly reported that in their opinion the sub-lessees of the penitentiary had not complied with the terms of the original contract between the State and the original lessees. Therefore "the original lessees have violated their contract with the State, having

---

honest laborers of Portland." See Statesman, September 22, 1862. Also the Governor's Special Message to the Legislature, September 15, 1862, Journal of the House, 1862, Appendix, pp. 46-49. Newell and English offered to give up their lease providing the state paid them for the improvements they had made. Statesman, October 22, 1860.

[13] Statesman, April 17, 1860.

[14] Oregonian, June 23, 1860.

[15] Journal of the House, 1860. p. 3.

[16] As a member of the committee on Indian affairs he assisted in the preparation of a memorial to Congress asking for payment of the cost of the Yakima Indian War.

[17] Ibid., p. 17.

failed to keep convicts according to the terms of their contract your committee recommend that the governor of the state be authorized by law to take charge of the penitentiary, and employ a warden and assistant warden to keep and superintend it."[18] Nothing was done until 1862.

Outside of his work on the two committees, Newell seems not to have been conspicuous at this session of the legislature. However, he was one of the few Democrats who voted for Edward D. Baker, a Republican, for United States Senator. Lane had pursued a pro-slavery course in Congress, which alienated many of his Democratic supporters in Oregon, though those who were his personal followers and those who agreed with his policies succeeded in electing nineteen to the legislature, while the Douglas Democrats secured only eighteen. The Lane or administration Democrats favored congressional intervention in the territories to permit slavery. The Douglas Democrats just as strongly avowed the doctrine of popular sovereignty. The break-up of the Democratic party over the issue left a balance of power with the Republicans who were greatly strengthened by the addition to their ranks of Colonel Edward D. Baker. Baker had come to Oregon with the one purpose of giving the Oregon Republicans a leader who could compare favorably with the Democratic leaders in the State.[19]

Jealousy and party rancor increased between the two wings of the Democratic party, until the Lane faction in the State senate absented themselves on several occasions to prevent legislation, their absence leaving no quorum.[20]

They also endeavored to prevent the election of a United States Senator by solidly backing Delazon Smith, who was absolutely unacceptable to the non-interventionist Douglas Democrats.[21] After many ballots failed to elect, the Douglas Democrats combined with the Republicans and elected Col. Edward Baker (he accepted the "popular sovereignty" doctrine) and J. W. Nesmith, a Douglas Democrat, as Senators to the United States Congress. Newell was one of fifteen Democrats who felt such a

---

[18] Journal of the House, 1860, Appendix, p. 10.
[19] See T. W. Davenport, "Slavery Question in Oregon," O.H.Q. (September 1908), IX:189-253, and Woodward, op. cit., pp. 106-188.
[20] Journal of the House, 1860; Statesman, October 8, 1860; Oregonian, October 6, 1860.
[21] Journal of the Senate of the Oregon Legislature, 1860, pp. 1-54.

combination was necessary and gave their reasons for so voting in a long article in the Statesman.[22] The slavery question so closely involved in Oregon's fight in Congress to become a State was an important factor in politics after acceptance into the Union.

The Willamette River Flood of 1861-1862

In December of 1861 the Willamette River rose to heights never before known by the settlers.[23] Amid large headlines telling of disaster, "Persons saved from trees, rafts and buildings," "Warehouse at Wheatland with 7000 bushels of Grain carried off," "15,000 bushels of wheat destroyed at Independence," and "Water flowing through Salem three feet deep," there is a little note stating

*Sternwheeler "Onward" being put to use during the Oregon Flood of 1861
Courtesy of the Special Collection at Salem Public Library, Salem, Oregon*

that "Dr. Newell reports that he has information of a great destruction of property and buildings at Champoeg."[24] The land along the river from Salem to Oregon City was in many places swept clean of improvements. Houses, barns, mills, storehouses and bridges gave way to the rampaging river. The water was over fifty feet above the low water level. The falls at Oregon City were

---

[22] Statesman, October 8, 1860. Also see Oregonian, October 6 and 12, 1860.
[23] Oregonian, December 14, 1861.
[24] Oregonian.

reduced to a ripple over which boats sailed.[25] Newell's information about the great destruction at Champoeg was not exaggerated. With the exception of his house, which was built on a hill out of danger of the flood, Newell lost all his possessions. His store, which housed the post office, and his large mill floated away, carrying with them the fruits of his labor and a large share of his fortune.[26]

The Robert Newell House in Champoeg, Oregon, circa 1900
Refuge for many families during the flood of December 1861
Reprinted with permission from the Oregon Historical Society

The loss had a noticeable effect upon Newell. Up to 1861 he had boasted that he had never asked anyone for a position.[27] But in the year of the flood he asked J. W. Nesmith to give him a position working with the Indians on the Yamhill Indian reservation. This letter contains passages, which show that the loss inflicted by the flood weighed heavily on Newell. The letter is written apologetically, with emphasis on the fact that it was the first time he had bothered anyone for an office and he was prompted to do so because of the flood and his inability to sell his farm.[28] Newell concludes with a paragraph reminding "friend Nez," as he addressed him, that Newell was a Nesmith supporter:

---

[25] Dobb, op. cit., p. 154. See Corning, op. cit., pp. 80-92.
[26] The house is not far from the historical marker in Champoeg. The writer journeyed to Champoeg to see the house, which is dilapidated and covered with vines but still standing.
[27] Statesman, July 17, 1860.
[28] Newell to Nesmith, January 13, 1861, Oregon Historical Society.

Now in conclusion let me say as we have spent the prime of our lives in this country and almost together in the ups and downs of life and should I have not in all respects done as was best in your opinion I believe you are willing to say let by gones be by gones and while I am for Douglas you may depend that I am a Nesmith man and a knowledge of your life since you come to Oregon leaves me to form this opinion of you. Oregon is safe in your hands.[29]

After reading this letter one cannot help pitying Newell who for years was able to hold a commanding position in his community because of his wealth, his personal leadership, and his activity in the government of the state. Now the flood had deprived him of most of his property and income and he was reduced to political backslapping and almost begging for some official position to defray his expenses. The days when he served as legislator and Speaker of the House were gone. The monopoly by which Newell, Crawford and Cook controlled transportation between Champoeg and Vancouver, with all the attendant prosperity, were also history. The wheel of fortune had turned for Robert Newell and it was necessary for him to find another means of livelihood. It is not surprising to find him seeking work among the Indians, for he felt himself qualified to give valuable service to the government by his experience with the red man.

---

[29] Ibid.

"Ghost Stores" at the re-located Champoeg, or Newellsville, circa 1939.
The structure on the left is said to be a pre-1861 saloon.
Reprinted with permission from the Oregon Historical Society
Portland, Oregon

Students standing in front of the Champoeg School prior to the 1861 flood.
This photo is the only known surviving photo taken of Champoeg before the flood of 1861.
Courtesy of the Champoeg State Heritage Area, Champoeg, Oregon

124

CHAPTER VIII

INDIAN AGENT: THE LAST YEARS

Nesmith evidently did not or could not secure for Newell the position desired because Newell wrote to him again on December 18, 1861, reporting that he had just returned from the Nez Perce country. Several persons had persuaded him to take a position as farmer on the Nez Perce Reservation, but he did this only for a short time, because in his own words, ". . . my services were required for something besides cultivating the soil."[1] While with the Indians Newell had observed that many of the miners from California were settling on lands owned by the Indians because there were insufficient soldiers to enforce the agreements made between the government and the Indians. The fault lay mainly with the white man, he thought, and if the situation were not remedied, "In a short time we will have another Indian war in that country and if such a thing should occur it will strip anything of the kind we have ever had on this coast."[2]

The Indian agency at Spalding, Idaho about 1867
Photo by Cummings – Courtesy Ira Dole
Reprinted with permission from the National Park Service,
Nez Perce National Historic Park

---

[1] Newell to Nesmith, December 18, 1861, Oregon Historical Society.
[2] Ibid.

Again in this letter Newell mentioned his financial misfortunes. Elliott states that Newell broke himself up in business helping his neighbors.[3] To Nesmith, Newell stated that "The citizens of this place are camped around here like a tribe of Indians, and my house is full of houseless neighbors."[4]

Until Newell decided to move his family to the Nez Perce country he commuted between his home and the Lapwai Indian agency at the Nez Perce Reservation in Idaho, acting at various times as interpreter and special commissioner.[5] At intervals he analyzed the Indian situation as it existed among the Nez Perces. The dominant theme in these letters and articles was Newell's strong sympathy with the Indians. Again and again he pointed out the failure of the government to carry out their agreements – the main reason, he thought, for the discontent and hostility of the Indians.[6]

Gold found in the Nez Perce Reservation interested Newell for a while. He wrote Nesmith that he was staying in the area "to see if anything can be made in the final wind up of this great gold excitement which is about passing away. There is just gold enough on this reservation to require some arrangement to be made between the whites and the Indians and no doubt it must be treaty or a war."[7] Again in this letter Newell asks for consideration that would secure his appointment as Indian agent at Lapwai: "If you can not consistently go with me in my request for Oneil as agent . . . Why not go for me." O'Neil was appointed, however, and Newell continued his search for a position. [8] All this time he was cementing friendship with the Indians by an honest effort to understand their problems. His efforts were not unnoticed by the Indians.

---

[3] Elliott, op. cit., p. 120.
[4] Newell to Nesmith, Champoeg, December 18, 1861..
[5] Dobbs, op. cit., p. 154; Elliott, op. cit., p. 121. Several letters from Newell to Nesmith mention his activity among the Indians during this period. These letters are in the Oregon Historical Society
[6] See Statesman, September 11, 1861, November 24, 1861; Newell to Nesmith, December 3, 1862.
[7] Newell to Nesmith, December 3, 1862, Oregon Historical Society.
[8] Newell wrote to Nesmith in 1863 that he understood why he had not been appointed. Newell said: I did get your first letter about my not being appointed, and have saw the law on the subject . . . All of which is satisfactory and politic."

When Idaho became a territory in 1863 it was necessary to negotiate with the Indians to acquire legal title to the land. In a treaty made in 1863 Newell's work among the Indians was officially recognized, for the Nez Perces refused to cede any land until the following article was inserted into the treaty:

> Inasmuch as the Indians in Council have expressed the desire that Robert Newell should have confirmed to him a piece of land lying between Snake and Clearwater rivers, the same having given to him on the 9th day of June 1861 and described in an instrument of writing bearing that date and signed by several chiefs of the tribe, it is hereby agreed that the said Robert Newell shall receive from the United States a patent for the said tract of land.[9]

In the same year Newell again entered the political arena, this time as an independent candidate. "Dr. Robert Newell of Lapwai announces himself this week as an independent candidate for Delegate to Congress from Idaho Territory. The Doctor is a union Democrat and we believe intends to run on that platform. Good for you old Champoeg! Go in and win. We don't believe the 'Gem of the Mountains' is likely to show better in any other hands."[10] When Wallace was nominated in October of 1863, Newell withdrew in order to "Unite all the Union men of the Territory."[11] This is the last time on record that Newell endeavored to acquire an elective position.

In 1863 two of Newell's sons died, Charles Newell, less than two years old, was drowned in a mill-race at Lapwai July 5, 1863.[12] Robert Newell, Jr., a son by Newell's Indian wife, was

---

[9] Charles Kappler, Indian Affairs, Laws and Treaties, 2 Vols. (Washington, D. C.: Government Printing office, 1904), II:847, Article 9. The complete treaty is also given. It was proclaimed in 1867. Newell did not move his family permanently until 1867. The Oregonian of March 6, 1867, noted his moving: "Dr. Robert Newell familiarly known as Bob Newell came down on the 'Alert' yesterday with his family enroute to Idaho. The doctor tells us he has sold his farm and 'traps' at Champoeg and is leaving the state for a new home."

[10] Oregonian, July 28, 1863.

[11] Statesman, October 26, 1863.

[12] Statesman, July 20, 1863.

killed by a man called "Frank" at Lewiston, Idaho, August 26, 1863.[13]

Newell again requested Nesmith to secure him the position of Indian agent in 1863, to no avail.[14] In a letter of January 30, 1863, he practically pleads with Nesmith to take note of his situation:

> I have been here over a year assisting inexperienced men done the talking with the Indians and I do believe I have prevented a muss among them . . . and as yet have not received a dollar in cash and I do believe if the Ind. department knew it they would see that I was paid for such services as 30 odd years experience can render the country. I . . . live within a few rods of the agency, go at all calls, and take an interest in the affairs of the agency. I have looked over a few sentences above and am rather sorry I have written it as it looks so much like I am begging but . . . here I am 55 years of age and doing what I can and still in hopes all will come out right . . . . I hate to trouble you but remember we are old Oregonians and have saw some service.

Though Newell apologized and tried not to sound as if he were begging, the letter clearly shows that he was using every method he could to impress Nesmith with his ability and convince him that he deserved the position, a far cry from Newell's former independence. But the coveted position did not come his way until 1868, after Newell had made a trip to Washington, D. C., to plead his own cause before President Johnson.

Before Newell left on his journey to Washington, his second wife, Rebecca Newman Newell, died. One of the eleven children she bore Newell, the second Robert Newell, Jr., was born fourteen

---

[13] Ibid., August 31, 1863. This boy was evidently a troublesome character. In 1862 he was involved in a gambling argument at Lapwai and severely wounded S. Wixson with a bowie knife. Ibid., December 8, 1863. Meek wrote to his son June 5, 1866, that Marcus Whitman, another of Newell's half breed children was hanged by a vigilance committee with David McLoughlin in March, 1866. Tobie, op. cit., p. 260.

[14] Newell to Nesmith, January 20, 1863.

days before her death. As in the case of his Indian wife, Newell made only a few remarks about Rebecca. In the family record there is a short note followed by Newell's initials: "Robert Newell Jr. was born 5th May 1867. His mother died on the 19th of the same month, was buried at Lewiston, Idaho Territory on the 20th of May 1867. May the Lord have mercy on her soul."[15]

The trip to Washington, D. C., was undertaken for two reasons. In order to facilitate a redivision of Indian lands, which had become necessary, Newell accompanied four of the Indian Chiefs and James O'Neil, the Indian agent, from Lapwai to Washington.[16] His desire to acquire O'Neil's position as Indian agent was no doubt the strongest motive for undertaking a journey so long and arduous. He described the first day of the trip as follows: "Left Lewiston I. T. at 7 o'clock in the morning horseback, fine weather. This was a lonesome day to me as I was alone and the idea of leaving my family for so long a journey and the place of destination seemed so far off."[17] This first day Newell rode forty miles, a strenuous journey for a man sixty-one years of age. He left on March 27th, boarded a steamer at The Dalles on March 31, and arrived in Portland at eight in the evening of the same day.

The steamer scheduled to take Newell from Portland to San Francisco did not leave Portland until April 10. During the interim he visited a few of his old friends and wrote some letters. His diary does not indicate that any antipathy existed between him and O'Neil, though one of the letters he wrote to Nesmith while waiting for the steamer contains an interesting and rather amusing statement: "I am sorry to think Oniel has not treated me right but as the Beaver said to the Otter we'll meet at the hatter shop."[18]

When the steamer John L. Stevens left Portland it was able to reach Astoria, but could go no further until the weather cleared. The ship waited in Astoria from Saturday until Monday, April 13, and then crossed the bar into the Pacific with some trouble. Newell

---

[15] Family Record, Appendix I. According to this record she died in the 35th year of her life. If this is correct she was only fourteen at the time she married Newell.

[16] Newell Diary, 1868. Newell kept a diary of his journey, which furnishes valuable information regarding his trip. From it we learn his religious preference; he attended the Episcopal Church whenever possible.

[17] Ibid.

[18] Newell to Nesmith, April 9, 1868, Oregon Historical Society. He was probably referring to the two being in Washington together.

reported that the "John L. Stevens had as much as she could do to live today," and the following day, "almost all seasick except myself."[19]

The party, consisting of Newell, O'Neil and the four Indians, arrived safely at San Francisco on April 16, and Newell spent some time with his old friend Peter H. Burnett and called several more of his acquaintances. He boarded the steamer <u>Montana</u> on April 21, and without further incident arrived in New York May 14.[20]

The wonders of the big city did not fail to impress Newell, who had spent most of his life in the wilderness and frontier settlements. "Arrived at our landing in New York truly a wonder. I went to the Metropolitan Hotel to the threatre, the grandest sight I ever saw."[21] The old mountain man was getting his first taste of the excitements of city life.

Robert Newell, 1868, during his stay in Washington D.C.
Reprinted with permission from the Oregon Historical Society, Portland, Oregon

---

[19] Newell Diary, 1868. April 13, 14.

[20] Newell left some interesting comments on prices aboard ship. Oranges were "25 cents a dozen, pineapples one bit a piece. Cigars 50 cents one hundred."

[21] Newell Diary, 1868, May 14.

For the most part Newell's account of his stay in Washington[22] is of little value for historical purposes, being mostly an account of his expenses, his health and the weather conditions. However, a few remarks give an insight into the political issues of the time. On May 16 he wrote: "Today the vote was taken on impeachment and lost, it was a day long to be remembered." His opinion of the people of Washington, D. C., was that they were "nearly all politicians and I think a tolerable hard set. The acquittal of the President is a sad affair to some and others are rejoicing." The 9th of July has this entry: "went to the capital and while there at the telegraph the wire brought news of the nomination of Seymore and soon after that of Blain. Many was dissapointed and some disgusted."

The Indians did not fare well in the city. Newell remarked several times that some of them were ill, although the weather was, in Newell's words, "Oregon like."

Newell was introduced to the President of the United States on May 20. He dismissed the event with one sentence: "Saw the President who paid me quite a compliment as a pioneer . . . I felt much flattered at the reception and bid him farewell."[23] Five days later one of the Indians, Ules-sen-ma-le-ken, died of typhoid fever.[24] He was buried the following day "at the 'Congressional Ground' four carriages attended by friends."

Negotiations between the Indians and the government lasted from May 27 to August 19. Again the diary is unfruitful regarding the actual negotiations. A typical entry reads as follows: "Saw Mr. Corbett with Oneil and Indians, quite a talk about our mission and non-compliance of treaty stipulations."[25]

The Indians petitioned the President to have Newell appointed agent of the Nez Perces. In response to this request the President sent Newell's name to the Senate for confirmation on July 22. The senate duly confirmed Newell, and on August 7 Newell gave bond to the government for $20,000 as Indian agent.[26] Following his appointment as commissioner, a treaty was completed

---

[22] He stayed only one day in New York and proceeded from there to Washington, D. C. Ibid, May 16.

[23] Newell Diary, May 20.

[24] Ibid., May 25.

[25] Ibid., June 8.

[26] Newell Diary, 1868, August 7.

on August 13, which Newell signed as "United States Agent," and the three Indian Chiefs, Lawyer, Timothy, and Jason, signed with their mark.[27]

Having received his appointment as Indian agent, Newell grew impatient to leave for home. Scarcely a day passed in which he failed to make note of the dilatory policies of the Indian Department: "getting tired of this place Washington City . . . Spent the day at the Indian Department done nothing our patience is nearly gone and for the best reasons. There seems to be no disposition to accommodate at our Indian Department. Every one is displeased who go there on business . . . ."[28]

At last on August 21 he left Washington for Idaho and arrived on September 22 after a strenuous overland trip.

His duties as Indian agent began on the 1st of October 1868.[29] While holding this position he acted with characteristic thoroughness. When he took over the agency the buildings, fencing, and saw-mill were in a dilapidated condition. There was insufficient lumber to repair them adequately, and the tools needed to make more lumber were either stolen or practically worthless. After some difficulty Newell secured fencing material and began the work of repairing the worn-out fences. A school was started in October, which drew students from as far as fifty miles away. Shortly after the school had made an encouraging start, small-pox appeared in the vicinity and at the request of the Indians the school was closed until the disease had subsided.

In April of 1869 the school was reopened with more students than had attended before, and by July 1 Newell wrote, "our school was in flattering progress."

A serious drought caused a failure in the wheat and oat crops and only one-third of the anticipated crop of corn and potatoes matured. The ground became so dry and hard that plowing was discontinued, as well as the saw-mill work.[30] This year proved a

---

[27] This Treaty is not mentioned in Newell's Diary. The treaty is given in Kappler, op. cit., II:1024, 1025. It was ratified February 24, 1869. It contained amendments to the treaty of 1863 regarding land allotment, money for teaching the Indians and preservation of forests on Indian land.
[28] Newell Diary, 1868, August 13.
[29] Ibid., October 1.
[30] The information pertaining to the work of the Lapwai agency was taken from Report of the commissioner of Indian affairs made to the Secretary of

difficult one for the reservation. To add to the hardships brought on by the drought the Indians were obtaining whisky from the white man. The Indians asked Newell to see that the practice was stopped, whereupon Newell wrote to Lieut. Charles Bendirie, commandant at Fort Lapwai, and asked that he send "twenty men or as many as you can spare to prevent the introduction or sale of liquors as required by law – you will oblige me by arresting any and all Indians found drunk and confine them in the guard-house so that we may find out who are the whisky venders."[31] Bendirie refused to send aid and Newell wrote a sharp reprimand in his report to the Indian Department, asking that such an inefficient man be removed from the Lapwai fort and stating that most of the trouble between the whites and the Indians could be avoided if the former could be forced to obey the terms of the treaty.[32] Due to a change in policy, however, the war department was placed in charge of Indian affairs,[33] and Newell was removed as Indian Agent on July 29, 1869. He was succeeded by Lieut. Wham of the United States Army, but only after President Grant had rejected a petition sent him by the Indians which stated that Newell had been their friend for over forty years and was the agent of their own choice, with a request that Grant retain him.[34]

Approximately one month before he was removed as agent Newell married his third wife, Mrs. Jane M. Ward.[35]

Had he continued as Indian agent he would have served only a short four months, for all his duties were ended on November 14, 1869, when he died of a heart attack at the age of sixty-two.

---

the Interior (Washington, D. C.: Government Printing Office, 1869), pp. 279-282.

[31] Ibid. Newell included an account of the incident in his report of 1869, with the letter he had written to Lieut. Bendirie.

[32] Ibid.

[33] Felix S. Cohen, Handbook of Federal Indian Law (Washington, D. C.: Government Printing Office, 1945), p. 18. Kappler, op. cit., p. 5. "After many years of charges against Indian Service field personnel of dishonesty and inefficiency a new system of choosing agents was inaugurated in 1868 under President Grant. Their nomination was for the most part delegated to various religious bodies active in missionary work . . . . The remaining agencies were filled by Army officers detailed for such duty." Cohen, p. 18.

[34] The petition is on file at Washington, D. C. See Elliott, op. cit., p. 123.

[35] June 25, 1869. Family Record, Appendix I.

Although he had served the Indians officially for about a year, the greater part of his life was spent in generous service and in a sincere attempt to be a friend who they could trust.

The Oregonian announced Newell's death on November 24: "We learn that Dr. Robert Newell died at Lewiston on Sunday November 14th . . . No one's name is more familiar to the people of Oregon that that of Dr. Newell."[36]

The Statesman, though it had printed many unpleasant lines about his political interests, was more eulogistic in its notice of his death:[37] "The old citizens of this valley and especially his old friends in this country where he resided for so many years will regret to hear of his death . . . . Dr. Robert Newell was a man of considerable information, of the most kindly heart and who had many friends. He had a natural insight into Indian character and was always influential among that race and much esteemed by them."[38]

The statements, which are extant about Newell from those who knew him, show that his genial, kind-hearted manner endeared him to many. There is a manuscript in the Bancroft Library signed by Jesse Applegate, which is a fitting epitaph to Newell's life:

> Though Newell came to the mountains from the state of Ohio in his youth he brought with him to his wild life some of the fruits of early culture, which he always retained. Though brave among the bravest he never made a reckless display of that quality and in the battlefields as in councils his conduct was always marked by prudence and good sense. Though fond of mirth and jollity and the life of social reunions he never degenerated from the instincts of a gentleman. Though his love of country amounted to a passion and his mountain life was spent in opposition and rivalry to the Hudson's

---

[36] Oregonian, November 24, 1869. This article states that Newell came to Oregon in 1835, an obvious error.

[37] Bush was no longer editor, he resigned in March, 1863. Woodward, op. cit., p. 219.

[38] Statesman, November 26, 1869. In a letter to the publisher of the Statesman Newell had indicated that he was not feeling well, but expected to be well again soon. The letter arrived one day before the news of his death. Ibid.

Bay Company, he never permitted his prejudices to blind his judgment, or by word or act do injustice to an adversary. Of undoubted truth and honor, he was the unquestioned leader and advisor of men of his class, both British and American and enjoyed to a great extent the confidence of all parties in the country. His influence in the early days was therefore great, and both in public and private life he was frequently called upon to exert it. It is enough to say in his praise that it was always exerted for good.[39]

Newell's name has been perpetuated in the name of a small creek east of Oregon City in Clackamas County, Newell Creek.[40] The successor to Champoeg, which was washed away in 1861, was called Newellsville. The town has never been large enough to become well known.[41] In 1943, in recognition of Champoeg Day, May 2, a liberty ship was launched at the Oregon Shipbuilding yards which was christened the Robert Newell in honor of his activity on that day in 1843.[42]

The honorable life which he lived is a lasting credit to his name, and Oregon can be proud that he was one of her founders, one who stood for honor and justice and conducted his business and political life with the same integrity.

In the words of J. W. Nesmith: "He has folded his robe about him and lain himself down to rest among the mountains he loved so well, and which have so often echoed the merry tones of his voice."[43]

Robert Newell may not have been one of the nation's great politicians or famous statesmen, but neither was he a mediocrity. Without the advantage of formal educational training, he made a rather remarkable name for himself as a mountain man, as legislator, as a businessman, and as a friend to the Indians.

---

[39] Oregon Voter, August 20, 1927. T. C. Elliott, op. cit., p. 108.

[40] Lewis A. McArthur, "Oregon Geographic Names," O.H.Q. (December, 1945), XLVI:345.

[41] Lloyd D. Black, "Middle Willamette Valley Population Growth," O.H.Q. (March, 1942) XLIII:49.

[42] Statesman, May 1, 1943.

[43] O.P.A.T. 1875, p. 6.

One is impressed with his good-natured kindliness, his generosity, his tolerance and his unbiased judgment. He was a staunch Democrat, yet his position on the capital location question and his vote for the Republican Colonel Baker show that he was not blinded to reality by party loyalty. Although he performed worthwhile service in the early legislature, he confessed his ignorance of jurisprudence. Probably his greatest service was as commissioner and agent to the Indians. His careful analysis of Indian troubles and his negotiations with the Indians show an understanding of and thorough acquaintance with the Indian nature. There may have been others who understood the Indian position as well as Newell, but very few frontier settlers extended to them the same tolerance, or were willing to recognize practically that an Indian had any rights.[44] Had our government been able to act in harmony with Newell's requests and appointed men of his experience and insight to the Indian agencies, a good many Indian wars might have been avoided, and a review of our Indian policy might have been less unpleasant to the historian.

---

[44] For example, see Harvey Scott's dictum in the Oregonian of June 26, 1877.

APPENDIX I

FAMILY RECORD OF ROBERT NEWELL

Document in possession Mrs. Augusta M. Wiggin, Lewiston, Idaho (Copy at Oregon Historical Society).

Robert Newell was married to his first wife 1833 July 27th.

Robert Newell was married to Rebecca Newman 28th June 1846.

Lott Wiggin was married to Mary Jane Newell 15th of March 1865.

Robert Newell married to Mrs. Jane M. Ward June 25th 1869.

Richard J. Monroe was married to Martha Ann Newell February 10th 1870.

Births

Robert Newell was born March 30th 1807

Rebecca Newman his wife, was born 20th May 1832

Albert Wiggin was born August 12th 1869
Charles Henery sic Wiggin was born Champoeg Oregon, Jan. 27th 1869
William Wiggin was born August 23, 1867, at Lapwai Agency, I. T.
Lott Edward Wiggin was born on the Pattit, W. T., Feb. 15, 1871
Mittie H. Wiggin was born on the Pattit, W. T., Jan. 1, 1873
John Wiggin was born at Lewiston, Feb. 3, 1875
Chester A. Wiggin was born at Lewiston Jan. 23, 1877
Died Lott Wiggin St., Dec. 22, 1898.

Robert Newell's children by his first wife

Francis Ermatinger Newell was born on Green River, South Pass,
    June 14, 1835.
William Moore Newell was born 30 March, 1838
Marcus Whitman Newell was born April 17, 1840
Robert Newell Jr was born Feb. 28, 1842.
Thomas Jefferson Newell was born Nov. 25, 1843.

Robert Newell's children by his second wife

James Henry Newell was born 21 September, 1847
Mary Jane Newell was born Nov. 26, 1849
Martha Ann Newell was born Feb. 11, 1852
Harvy Simms Newell was born August 2, 1854
Samuel Newell was born July 23, 1856
Harriet Newell was born Dec. 19, 1859
George Edward Newell was born January 26, 1861
Charles Newell was born January 2, 1862
Stephen Douglas Newell was born Feb. 29, 1864
Lott Newell was born March 11, 1866.
Robert Newell Jr. was born May 5, 1867.
    (His mother died on the 19th of the same month, and
    (was buried at Lewiston, Idaho Territory on May 20, 1867
    (May the Lord have mercy on her soul.

Deaths

James Henry Newell died 24th June 1848
George Edward Newell died 2nd March 1861, he was five weeks old.
Charles Newell died July 5th 1863
Lott Newell died June 23rd 1866
Albert Wiggin died January 25th 1870
Martha Ann Monroe died at Lewiston Idaho March 30th 1874
    in sic
Charles H. Wiggin died November 13th 1888
Lott Wiggin died Dec. 22nd 1898
Richard J. Monroe 56 year of age Sept. 24 1867

William Moore Newell died March 29th 1855
Robert Newell Jr. died August 23rd 1863

Rebecca Newell – Robert Newell's second wife died 20 <u>sic</u> May
1867
Rebecca Wife of Robert Newell Sen died at Lewiston Idaho
Territory May 19th A. D. 1867 in the 35th year of her
age.

ROBERT NEWELL Sen Died Nov 14th A. D. 1869 in the 63rd
year of his age.

BIBLIOGRAPHY

Reference

Guide to the Manuscript Collections of the Oregon Historical Society, prepared by the Oregon Historical Records Survey, Division of Professional and Service Projects, Historical Survey, 1940.

Oregon State Documents, A Checklist, 1843 to 1925, compiled by Eleanor R. Rockwood, Portland: Binford and Mort, for the Oregon Historical Society.

Pacific Northwest Americans, A Checklist of Books and Pamphlets Relating to the Pacific Northwest, compiled by Charles W. Smith, New York: The H. W. Wilson Company, 1921.

Primary Sources

Manuscripts

Applegate, Jesse, MS in Bancroft Library, University of California, Berkeley, giving his estimate of Newell.

Griffin, John S., MS, "Provisional and Territorial Papers of Oregon," No. 1711, Oregon Historical Society.

Minto, John, "Hearing the Cry of the Wild," MS, Oregon Historical Society.

Newell, Robert, "Account of Champoeg Meeting," MS 448, Oregon Historical Society.

_____. Annotations in Copy of Grover's Oregon Archives in Bancroft Library, Microfilm, Oregon Historical Society.

_____. "Agreement Between Newell and Alvin T. Smith," MS 186, Oregon Historical Society.

_____. "Capital Location Proposal," MS 677, Oregon Historical Society.

_____. "Correspondence to the Herald," MS 979.1, Oregon
Historical Society. These articles published in the Oregon
Herald, a Portland newspaper printed first on March 17,
1866, and ceased in publication in 1873. The original
correspondence rather than the printed articles in the Herald
have been used.

Original Minutes of the Oregon Lyceum Club, MSS 655, 655.10,
and 655.04, Oregon Historical Society.

Precinct Report of Marion County, 1854, MS 199.5, Oregon
Historical Society.

T'Vault, William G., to the Board of Directors of the Oregon
Printing Association, MS 655, pp. 1-25, Oregon Historical
Society.

Waldo, Daniel, "Critiques," MS 313, Oregon Historical Society.

United States Government Publications

Cohen, Felix S., Handbook of Federal Indian Law, Washington,
D. C.: Government Printing Office, `945.

Congressional Globe, August 13, 1848, 30th Congress, 1st session.

Kappler, Charles, editor and compiler, Indian Affairs, Laws and
Treaties, 2 volumes, Washington, D. C.: Government
Printing Office, 1904.

Report of the Commissioner of Indian Affairs, 1869, Washington,
D. C.: Government Printing Office, 1870.

Treaties and Conventions Concluded Between the United States
of America and Other Powers Since July 4, 1776,
Washington, D. C.: Government Printing Office, 1889.

U. S. Census, Schedule 1, Report for Marion County, 1850,
Government Report on Production of Agriculture in
Marion County Territory of Oregon, 1850.

U.S. Census for 1850, typed copy, Marion Country census,
Oregon Historical Society.

House and Senate Documents

House Executive Document No. 1, 31st Congress, 2nd session,
Series No. 595, pp. 156-168.

House Executive Document No. 104, 32nd Congress, 1st session,
Series No. 648 (Article 2), P. 6.

House Executive Document No. 104, 32nd Congress, 1st session,
Series No. 648 (Article 3), pp. 7-24.

House Executive Document No. 38, 35th Congress, 1st session,
Series 955, pp. 2-66.

Senate Executive Document No. 52, 31st Congress, 1st session,
Vol. 13.

Oregon Publications

Biennial Messages of Governor L. F. Grover to the Legislative
Assembly of the State of Oregon, Eighth Session, 1874,
Salem: Martin V. Brown, State Printer, 1874.

Grover, LaFayette, The Oregon Archives, including the Journals,
Governors' Messages and Public Papers of Oregon, Salem:
Asahel Bush, Public Printer, 1853.

Journal of the House of Representatives, Oregon Legislature,
Salem: Asahel Bush, Territorial Printer, December 1, 1851.

Journal of the Proceedings of the House of the Legislative
Assembly of Oregon, sessions of 1859, 1860, 1861, and
1862, Salem: State Printer.

Journal of the Proceedings of the Senate of the Legislature
    Assembly of Oregon During the First Regular Session
    Thereof Begun September 10, 186-, Salem: Asahel Bush,
    State Printer, 1860.

Newspapers

Oregon Journal, Portland, Oregon, for: March 22, 1925; September 10,
    1932.

Portland Oregonian, Portland, Oregon, for: December 6, 1851; February
    14, 1852; June 26, 1852; May 8, 1854; October 6, 1860; May 1,
    1861; May 20, 1861; July 28, 1863; March 6, 1867; November
    24, 1869; November 29, 1869; February 4, 1888; November 11,
    1900; November 18, 1900; and May 3, 1901.

Oregon Statesman, Salem, Oregon, for: March 28, 1851; May 2, 1851;
    December 30, 1851; January 6, 1852; June 29, 1852; March 28,
    1854; April 4, 1854; April 10, 1855; February 16, 1858; March
    9, 1858; June 22, 1858; March 29, 1859; June 21, 1859;
    September 20, 1859; March 6, 1860; April 17, 1860; May 1,
    1860; July 17, 1860; October 8, 1860; October 22, 1860;
    September 11, 1861; November 24, 1861; October 26, 1863;
    and July 20, 1863.

Spectator, Oregon City, Oregon, for: February 19, 1846; April 2, 1846;
    April 16, 1846; April 30, 1846; September 17, 1846; November
    12, 1846; December 10, 1846; December 24, 1846; March 18,
    1847; May 27, 1847; June 24, 1847; December 9, 1847;
    December 10, 1847; December 25, 1847; January 6, 1848;
    January 20, 1848; February 10, 1848; April 6, 1848; July 13,
    1848; October 28, 1851, and March 16, 1851.

Letters

Boise, Reuben P., to Asahel Bush, May 1, 1851, Oregon Historical
    Society.

Deady, Matthew P., to Asahel Bush, May 4, 1851, Oregon Historical
    Society.

Eddy, Chauncey, to David Greene, February 17, 1836, cited in Clifford
    M. Drury, Henry Harmon Spalding, p. 129.

Newell, Robert, to Addison C. Gibbs, July 7, 1865.

Newell to Nesmith, January 13, 1861; December 18, 1861; December 3, 1862; and April 9, 1868.

Newell to Lane, February 1, 1852, and April 10, 1852.

Rich, E. E., (Ed.), <u>The Letters of John McLoughlin From Fort Vancouver to the Governor and Committee</u>, Toronto, Canada: The Champlain Society, 1944, Third Series.

Spalding, H. H., to Greene, October 15, 1842. Letters of the American Board, as cited in Drury, <u>Henry Harmon Spalding</u>, p. 198.

Diaries, Reminiscences, Records and Addresses

Case, William., "Reminiscences of William M. Case," in <u>Oregon Historical Quarterly</u> (September, 1900, I:269-295.

Donation Land Claim, No. 2051.

Hastings, Lansford W., "Documentary," <u>Oregon Historical Quarterly</u> (June, 1901), II:186-203.

Lee, Daniel, "Reminiscences of Daniel Lee," Microfilm in the Oregon Historical Society. The writer had access to the original as it was being microfilmed in the Society at Portland.

Lovejoy, Asa L., "Lovejoy's Pioneer Narrative, 1842-1848," <u>Oregon Historical Quarterly</u> (June, 1930), XXXI:237-260.

Matthieu, F. D., "Reminiscences of F. D. Matthieu," <u>Oregon Historical Quarterly</u> (March, 1900), I:73-104.

Newell, Robert, Family Record, Vertical File, Oregon Historical Society.

_____. Diary of 1829. This diary is an account of Newell's trapping experience in the mountains. The diary begins in 1829 and ends with the year 1842. There are several copies of the original. The University of Oregon Library possesses a microfilm copy. As the pages of the original are not numbered and the copies follow different forms, the page numbers have not been designated in the footnotes.

_____. Diary of 1868. Newell's trip to Washington, D. C., is described in this diary, a copy of which is in the Oregon Historical Society in Portland.

Original Minutes of the Champoeg Lodge No. 27, A. F. and A. M.

Provisional and Territorial Papers of Oregon, Nos. 12186. 12191, 12203, 1096, 913, and 1744. These papers contain the same material as Grouer's Oregon Archives, except they are far more complete. The Oregon Historical Society has both the original papers and a microfilm copy. Numbers cited refer to the original.

Russel, Osborne, Journal of a Trapper, from the original manuscript, 1834-1843, Boise, Idaho: Syms-York, Co., 1921.

Smith, Alvin T., Diary, original in the Oregon Historical Society. The entries in the diary are compact and written in small letters to conserve space. It has been used chiefly to substantiate dates.

Thurston, Samuel R., "Diary," Oregon Historical Quarterly (September, 1914), XV:137-205.

Transactions of the Oregon Pioneer Association

"Copy of a Document Found Among the Private Papers of the late Dr. John McLoughlin," 1880, pp. 46-55.

"History of the Provisional Government of Oregon," by J. Q. Thornton, 1874, pp. 42-96.

"Occasional Address," by Col. J. W. Nesmith, 1875, pp. 42-62.

"Annual Address," by Col. J. W. Nesmith, 1800, pp. 8-27.

"Annual Address," by Hon. William Strong, 1878, pp. 13-28.

"Annual Address," by S. F. Chadwick, 1874, pp. 15-32.

Books

Burnett, Peter H., Recollections and Opinions of an Old Pioneer,
New York: D. Appleton and Co., 1880.

Chittenden, Hiram M., and Richardson, D. T., The Life, Letters and
Travels of Father Pierre-Jean De. Smet, 4 volumes, New York:
Francis P. Harper, 1904.

Evans, Elwood, History of the Pacific Northwest: Oregon and
Washington, 2 volumes, Portland: North Pacific History
Company, 1889.

Gray, William H., History of Oregon, Portland: Harris and Holman,
1870.

Hastings, Lansford W., A New Description of Oregon and California,
Cincinnati: Quaker City Publishing House, 1857.

Hines, Gustavus, Wild Life in Oregon, New York: Worthington
Company, 1881.

Irving, Washington, The Rocky Mountains: Digested from the Journal
of Captain Bonneville, 2 volumes, Philadelphia: Lea and
Blanchard, 1837.

McBeth, Kate C., The Nez Perces Since Lewis and Clark, New York:
Fleming H. Renell Company, 1908.

Thornton, J. Quinn, Oregon and California in 1848, New York: Harper
Brothers, 1855.

White, Elijah, Ten Years in Oregon, compiled by Miss A. J. Allen, Ithaca,
New York: Andrus, Gauntlet and Co., 1850.

Secondary Sources

Books

Brown, Henry J., <u>Political History of Oregon</u>, Portland, Oregon: Wiley
    B. Allen, Publisher, Press of the Lewis and Dryden Printing
    Company, 1892.

Carey, Charles H., <u>A General History of Oregon Prior to 1861</u>, 2 volumes,
    Portland: Metropolitan Press, 1935.

Carey, Charles H., <u>The Oregon Constitution and Proceedings and Debate
    of the Constitutional Convention of 1858</u>, Salem: State Printing
    Department, 1926.

Clark, Dan Elbert, <u>The West in American History</u>, New York: Thomas Y.
    Crowell, 1937.

Clark, Robert C., <u>History of the Willamette Valley, Oregon</u>, Chicago:
    S. D. Clarke Publishing Co., 1927.

Clarke, S. A., <u>Pioneer Days of Oregon History</u>, Portland: J. K. Gill, 1905.

Corning, Howard McKinley, <u>Willamette Landings, Ghost Towns of the
    River</u>, Portland: Binford and Mort, 1947.

Dobbs, Caroline, <u>Men of Champoeg</u>, Portland: Metropolitan Press, 1932.

Drury, Clifford M., <u>Henry Harmon Spalding</u>, Caldwell, Idaho: The Caxton
    Printers, 1937.

Hines, H. K., <u>An Illustrated History of the State of Oregon</u>, Chicago: The
    Lewis Publishing Company, 1893.

Holman, Frederick V., <u>Dr. John McLoughlin, the Father of Oregon</u>,
    Cleveland: A. H. Clark Company, 1907.

Johnson, Robert C., <u>John McLoughlin: Patriarch of the Northwest</u>,
    Portland: Metropolitan Press, 1935.

Lyman, Horace S., <u>History of Oregon, the Growth of an American State</u>,
    4 volumes, New York: North Pacific Publishing Society, 1903.

FROM THE AUTHOR

Dear Friend,

Writing this thesis sparked a life long interest in research mainly because the Oregon Historical Society allowed me to enter their inner sanctum where there were hundreds of letters, diaries and documents in their original form. It was truly fascinating experience writing from so many original sources.

My wife and I have been married 63 years, and are proud parents of four children. Dorthy has been a tremendous help in every avenue of life, even writing this thesis.

School teaching has been my vocation for twenty-eight years, and I never went to school one day without enjoying it, and being thankful for having chosen that vocation.

Our interests now are our grandchildren, and a large ranch in central Oregon near Paulina.

George Guy Delamarter